THE MEN WHO RAISED
THE BAR

THE MEN WHO RAISED THE BAR

The evolution of the highest individual score in Test cricket

Chris Waters

WISDEN
LONDON · OXFORD · NEW YORK · NEW DELHI · SYDNEY

WISDEN
Bloomsbury Publishing Plc
50 Bedford Square, London, WC1B 3DP, UK

First published in Great Britain 2020

www.wisden.com
www.wisdenrecords.com
Follow Wisden on Twitter @WisdenAlmanack
and on Facebook at Wisden Sports

A catalogue record for this book is available from the British Library

Library of Congress Cataloguing-in-Publication data has been applied for

ISBN: HB: 978-1-4729-7753-3; eBook: 978-1-4729-7755-7

2 4 6 8 10 9 7 5 3 1

Typeset in Stempel Garamond Roman by Deanta Global Publishing Services,
Chennai, India
Printed and bound in Great Britain by CPI Group (UK) Ltd, Croydon CR0 4YY

To find out more about our authors and books visit www.wisden.com
and sign up for our newsletters

To the record holders, for the pleasure that they
gave and the lives that they inspired

Contents

Charles Bannerman (165*)
Australia versus England
Melbourne 1877

Strictly speaking Charles Bannerman was not one of *The Men Who Raised the Bar*. The Australian batsman *set* the bar, leaving it next to "165", a record that stood for seven years. Bannerman's score in the very first Test gave the record the perfect start. He faced the opening ball of the game, the story neatly beginning with him. Strictly speaking too, Bannerman did not perform his feat in a Test, or know at the time he'd set a record. The match was between a combined Melbourne/Sydney XI and James Lillywhite's touring team and only later termed "Australia v England". In 1894, Clarence Moody, an Adelaide journalist, wrote in his book *Australian Cricket and Cricketers* a list of what he considered "Test matches". This was accepted by Charles Alcock, the Surrey CCC secretary and leading English authority, and so was born – with glorious quaintness – the glorious tradition of Test cricket.

Under different circumstances, Bannerman might have been playing for England. He was born in Woolwich, London, in 1851, the son of William Bannerman, a Scotsman, and his wife, Margaret, who came from Ireland. When Charles was two, the Bannermans emigrated when his father – a lance-corporal in the Royal Sappers and Miners at the Royal Arsenal, Woolwich – was posted to Sydney. The British government had set up a Sydney branch of the Royal Mint to counter a black market in gold at the height of the gold rush, and Bannerman worked in the Mint as a blacksmith. He'd been in Australia for six years when he suddenly died, aged 40, after an attack of *delirium tremens* (DTs), a condition normally caused by alcohol withdrawal. It left Charles's mother with seven children to support including his younger brother, Alec, who also played for Australia.

Charles Bannerman played his earliest cricket at Sydney's Warwick Cricket Club, a stone's throw from the Sydney Mint. He was taught by Billy Caffyn, a famous Surrey and England all-rounder, who'd stayed in Australia after touring as a player. Practices were staged in the shadow of the Mint where the teenage Charles worked as a mechanic. Bannerman, however, had no time for the job and was cocky and rebellious in his youth. In 1871, one month before his 20th birthday, he was sacked from the Mint "having persistently neglected his duty, notwithstanding repeated warnings and opportunities of amendment and having moreover been guilty of insolence to his superior officer and general insubordination". He had a temper too, quitting Warwick CC in a huff to join East Sydney when one of his team-mates earned more than he did for making a big score. The *Sydney Mail* criticised his childishness, insisting that he was "so spoiled and petted" by his early cricketing success that he "lost his head". Bannerman returned to Warwick a year later and he also represented New South Wales, who then played infrequently against Victoria, then the only other Australian first-class opposition. In the weeks before the first Test,

Bannerman played a key role in two wins achieved by New South Wales XVs against James Lillywhite's tourists that first gave rise to the idea – hitherto thought absurd – that Australians could challenge their English counterparts in 11-a-side games. Until then, it was not felt that an Australian XI would be strong enough to compete on equal terms with the English, who often played against up to 22 players to make a game of it. But the success of Bannerman and his colleagues helped inspire a "Grand Combination Match" (the official title of the first Test), which featured 11 players from Victoria/New South Wales (Melbourne/Sydney) against Lillywhite's men.

The "Grand Combination Match" was not fully representative of Australia or England, with neither side at maximum strength. Internal politics undermined local preparations, with star fast bowler Fred "The Demon" Spofforth refusing to play because he disapproved of the

Melbourne Cricket Ground prepares for the "Grand Combination Match", later classed as the inaugural Test.

choice of wicketkeeper. Frank Allan, Spofforth's replacement, pulled out to attend an agricultural fair. For their part, England were missing a raft of leading amateurs including star batsman W. G. Grace, with the tourists made up solely of professionals. In addition, their preparation for the Test was somewhat different to the modern routine of pre-match practice days and careful planning. They arrived in Melbourne less than 24 hours before the start of the match after a fraught, six-week sojourn in New Zealand where they had frequent brushes with death in some of the most primitive travelling conditions imaginable. Several players almost drowned while crossing Otira Gorge on South Island, while hair-raising stagecoach journeys threatened life and limb. The side that lined up against Bannerman and co on Thursday, March 15, 1877, for the first Test was shattered and still suffering the after-effects of seasickness (Tom Armitage, a tall and strapping Yorkshire all-rounder, was reportedly so ill that he was barely able to stand up). Nor was it simply a case of leaving him out or any of his colleagues. With every penny eating into profits, the squad consisted of just 12 players, meaning little rest whether fit or not.

By the time that England got to Melbourne, they were down to the bare bones of 11 after wicketkeeper Ted Pooley had been thrown in jail. Pooley bet a man named Ralph Donkin that he could predict the score of each member of the local 18 in a match against the tourists in Christchurch, nominating nought as each man's figure. Sure enough, a generous number of ducks ensued, leading to a handsome profit. However, Donkin refused to pay and a scuffle took place, resulting in Pooley's arrest and that of Alf Bramall, the touring team's baggage man. Pooley and Bramall were charged with damaging Donkin's property and kept in

New Zealand pending trial. Their case was not heard until over a fortnight after the Test, whereupon both were acquitted. Considering them hard done to, the locals raised £50 and presented a gold watch to Pooley, who returned to England alone.

In Pooley's absence, and with reserve wicketkeeper Harry Jupp suffering "inflammation of the eyes", the short and thickset Nottinghamshire batsman John Selby was pressed into service behind the stumps. Jupp, a broad-shouldered Surrey batsman nicknamed "Young Stonewaller", still had to play because there was nobody else. The rest of

The England team at Priory Park, Chichester, before sailing Down Under. Standing (l-r): Harry Jupp, Tom Emmett, Arthur Hobgen (financial backer), Allen Hill, Tom Armitage. Sitting (l-r): Ted Pooley, James Southerton, James Lillywhite (captain), Alfred Shaw, George Ulyett, Andrew Greenwood. In front (l-r): Harry Charlwood, John Selby.

the side was made up of five Yorkshiremen in the form of the seasick Armitage; the tall pace bowler and hard-hitting batsman George Ulyett; the wiry left-arm quick and attacking batsman Tom Emmett; the diminutive strokeplayer Andrew Greenwood, and the strong right-arm fast bowler Allen Hill. Sussex had two representatives – pint-sized Harry Charlwood, a hard-hitting, free-scoring batsman and James Lillywhite himself, a slow and steady left-arm bowler. Short and stocky, with bushy beard, Lillywhite came from a famous cricketing family and was player/captain/manager/tour promoter rolled into one. Alfred Shaw, who assisted him in his managerial role, was another short and stocky fellow. The Nottinghamshire slow-medium bowler was one of the most accurate of all time, sending down more overs in his career than he conceded runs. The attack was completed by Surrey slow bowler James Southerton, who remains the oldest Test debutant at 49.

On a sunny Melbourne day, not too hot with a freshening breeze, the Australians won the toss and chose to bat. The Englishmen took to the field in "cloth caps and ties splashing colour", and there were about 1,000 spectators. Play began at 1.05pm but, according to the *Melbourne Argus*, "a number of persons were on the ground several hours before that time, misled by the announcement which we were inadvertently led to make through the misinterpretation of some curiously-written figures in a short notice supplied to us on Thursday". The paper added, in a flimsy attempt to make light of its blunder, that the start-time "seemed a late hour to begin a game that was to be stopped at five, especially when half-an-hour had to be deducted for luncheon at two o'clock. Practically it left only three hours for play, and the question naturally suggested itself whether life is not too short to permit of such spendthrift waste of an autumn day". The Melbourne ground had a new grandstand, but most spectators preferred to sit on the lawn embankment or on wooden seats in front of the cycle track. The eucalyptus trees in Yarra Park, in which the ground is sited, bore a number of "free onlookers", one of whom "dropped from his free seat in one of the eucalypti and had to be admitted into the Melbourne Hospital soon afterwards".

Alfred Shaw opened the bowling from the eastern end to Charles Bannerman, who scored Test cricket's first run when he cut the second ball past point (newspapers made no mention of the first delivery). Like his Australian rival, Shaw's place in history was thus assured by his involvement in that opening exchange. Like his Australian rival too, Shaw had come to cricket after being sacked from his first job of work – that of a human scarecrow in his home village of Burton Joyce in Nottinghamshire. In a bid to avert the mind-numbing tedium, which involved blowing a horn and wielding clappers, Shaw and a fellow scarecrow deserted their posts to play cricket. The youngsters were found by the angry farmer, whose wheat had been scoffed by a swarm of rooks. "There was no excuse for such a dereliction of duty," wrote Shaw. "That night I accepted my week's wage and, with it, my discharge."

Bannerman's opening partner was Nat Thomson, his New South Wales team-mate who was bowled by Hill in the fourth over. Tom Horan, a powerful all-rounder who became a famous cricket writer under the pen-name "Felix", hit the first boundary when he fortuitously edged Hill through the slips. With the score on 40, Horan was bounced out by a quicker one from Shaw, who had him taken by Hill at third man. The Combined side slipped to 41 for three when the six-foot tall, bushy-bearded captain Dave Gregory – said to have borne a striking resemblance to the infamous bushranger Ned Kelly – ran himself out, whereupon lunch was taken after 55 minutes with Bannerman on 27. After lunch, which ran ten minutes over in more "spendthrift waste of an autumn day", Bannerman and Bransby Cooper stabilised the hosts on a pitch that the tourists said was of English standard. The crowd, now numbering around 3,000 and later climbing to about 4,500, included, said one report, "a numerous company of the youth and beauty of Melbourne, many of whom seemed to take more than a passing interest in the game".

Cooper, who'd been born in India and attended Rugby School in England, was a stylish batsman and the most experienced member of the home XI (he'd played for Middlesex and Kent before emigrating in 1869). He gave as much strike as possible to Bannerman, who started to play with growing freedom, especially in the arc between mid-on and mid-off. In an era when most leading batsmen played from the crease, content to let the ball come to them, Bannerman was unusual in that he often advanced towards it, even against the quicker bowlers. Charles Beal, who managed the Australian sides in 1882 and 1888, described him as "a quick-footed hitter", saying: "He would jump in like a cat and biff would go the ball on the off or on the straight drive. He could hit the ball as hard as any man I ever knew, but he did not go in for lofting the ball." Bannerman described himself as "a forcing batsman – not a mere slogger".

Physically he packed a powerful punch at 5ft 7½in and 11 stone five pounds. Tom Garrett, his pace-bowling team-mate, who made the next-highest score in the innings of 18 not out from No. 9, branded him "a pocket Hercules". Bannerman was athletic and played a number of sports; he was an accomplished runner, a fair amateur rower (albeit "subject to cramp") and a useful swimmer and billiard player. In a rare personal recollection of him, the Australian cricketer-turned-journalist Jack Worrall remembered Bannerman's "big blue eyes" and "lisp".

Alfred Shaw wrote in his memoirs that Bannerman was dropped off his bowling by Armitage at mid-off before he'd got to double figures, but no newspaper mentioned it. Shaw said that "the ball was lobbed up in the simplest style and hit Armitage in the stomach". So out of sorts was the seasick Armitage, a normally useful slow-medium bowler, that he could manage only three overs which, in those days, consisted of four balls. One of his offerings sailed so high

Charles Bannerman: the man who set the bar.

over Bannerman's head, and the next so pathetically along the ground, that one account said that "the crowd was shaking with laughter, as nothing like this had ever been seen in the Colonies before". Nothing like Bannerman's play had ever been seen in the Colonies either, at least not from an Australian. *The Australasian* called it "the grandest display of batting by a colonial player which has ever been seen", adding that "Grace himself could not have batted with more resolution and greater brilliance than Bannerman of Sydney". The paper said that Bannerman "hit with decision, sharpness and vigour" and that the "constancy with which the ball was sent along the turf showed that caution and accuracy were allied to enterprise". James Lillywhite said that although he had seen as good an innings before in England, he had seen none better.

The post-lunch session was the second and last of day one, Bannerman scoring another 99 runs to reach 126 out of 166 for six at stumps. He'd lost Cooper with the total on 118, bowled by Southerton, and all-rounder Billy Midwinter with the score on 142, caught on the boundary by Ulyett off Southerton. Ned Gregory, brother of captain Dave, had registered Test cricket's first duck when he was caught at long-on by Greenwood off Lillywhite, which had left the hosts 143 for six. Bannerman, however, had ploughed on skilfully, reaching his fifty in two hours, ten minutes and raising his century just half-an-hour later to "clapping hands all around the ring". According to the *Melbourne Argus*, Bannerman almost perished for 87 when he hit a low skimming drive off Southerton to Shaw, who had "the chance to earn a glorious name". However, "desperate a rush as he [Shaw] made for the ball, he only reached it with the tips of his fingers." The paper added: "He [Shaw] says the light spoiled his sight... The catch was possible, and we should have been very sorry to have seen it offered to so dexterous a fieldsman as Emmett." Just as newspapers made no mention of Shaw's claim that Armitage dropped Bannerman off his bowling before he'd reached double figures, so Shaw's memoirs made no mention that he himself dropped Bannerman. Play ended at five o'clock after three hours, 15 minutes' cricket with wicketkeeper Jack Blackham unbeaten on three.

Day two began at 12.45pm in cool and cloudy weather before a crowd of around 3,000. Blackham was the only wicket in the pre-lunch session, Southerton bowling him for 17 as the Combined side reached 230 for seven at the break (Bannerman 159). When the total was 240, however, Bannerman was struck a painful blow on the second finger of his right hand by Ulyett as he tried to turn a short ball to leg. Although Bannerman was wearing batting gloves, the India rubber had worn away at the point of impact and he was forced to retire hurt for 165. The *Melbourne Argus* said that Ulyett had been "pitching his cannon shots not more than halfway down", and Bannerman suffered a smashed nail. The innings subsided as left-arm spinner Tom Kendall was caught in the slips by Southerton off Shaw, who then bowled left-arm pace bowler John Hodges for a duck as the hosts ended on 245.

Bannerman had batted for four-and-three-quarter hours and his innings included 35 singles, 14 twos, ten threes and 18 fours. Eleven of his boundaries were scored between wide mid-off and wide mid-on, four in front of point, two in front of square leg and one to third man. His hundred was the first by an Australian against English opposition, the highest Test score in Australia until Syd Gregory's 201 in the 1894 Sydney Ashes Test and it remains the highest by an Australian on Test debut. Incredibly, Bannerman's percentage of his side's runs (67.34) also remains the highest in a completed Test innings.

Bannerman couldn't field due to the injury and watched from the pavilion as his team-mates dismissed the tourists for 196 to take a shock lead of 49. It would have been even worse for the English had umpires Curtis Reid and Richard Terry noticed that Jupp, the "Young Stonewaller", had trod on his stumps before he'd scored. Jupp's inflamed eyes might have prevented him from keeping wicket but they weren't so badly affected that he couldn't open the batting and top-score with 63. The pick of the bowlers was Midwinter, one of six non-Australian-born players in the home XI who took five for 78 with his medium pace. In addition to playing eight Test matches for Australia, Midwinter played four for England before meeting a desperately sad fate. Unhinged by the sudden death of his wife and two children, he died in a lunatic asylum, aged 39.

Despite his injury, which had scarcely improved, Bannerman opened the hosts' second innings and received a rousing reception from a day three Saturday crowd of around 12,000. It was "as lovely a day for cricket as Melbourne ever enjoyed", with bright sunshine and a light breeze, and the new grandstand was almost full. Bannerman played out the opening over from Shaw, a maiden, and then got off the mark by driving Shaw to the mid-on boundary. However, he was "very cramped and showing the effects of his injury" and had not added to his score when he was bowled by Ulyett, of whom it was said he seemed nervous after what happened to him in the first innings. With Bannerman gone, the hosts were dismissed for 104, Horan top-scoring with 20 and Shaw returning five for 38. Chasing 154 (an apparent formality considering their strength), the English were sensationally skittled for 108. Tom Kendall, born in Bedford, wreaked havoc on the country of his birth by taking seven for 55 with his left-arm spin. Some thought that the visitors' run-chase on a warm fourth day, watched by around 3,000, was not assisted by a copious lunch and considerable quantities of beer. Remarkably, the 45-run victory margin was repeated by Australia in the Centenary Test against England at Melbourne in 1977.

After the Combined team's famous triumph, the Australian press was suitably crowing. *The Australasian* said that the tourists were the weakest side to have visited the Colonies – "notwithstanding the presence among them of Shaw, who is termed the premier bowler of England". The paper added: "If Ulyett, Emmett and Hill are fair specimens of the best fast bowling in England, all we can say is, either they have not been in their proper form in this Colony or British bowling has sadly deteriorated." Shaw offered no excuse for the tourists' loss. "For the time being," he wrote, "the defeated Englishmen and their associates in the Colonies had to be content to eat humble pie – sweetened, it is true, with the thought that it was members of their own race who had offered it, but humble pie all the same."

The success of the "Grand Combination Match" inspired a "Return Combination Match" in Melbourne a fortnight later, subsequently classed as the second Test. Bannerman was passed fit to open after Dave Gregory again won the toss and chose to bat. Bannerman scored ten in 55 minutes before playing on to Hill, the Combined team making 122. On the face of it, Bannerman's was an uncharacteristically stodgy innings but the *Melbourne Argus* made clear: "Though he showed no inclination to hit hard, nothing could be finer to look at than the stubborn defence he maintained against the puzzling assaults of Shaw." After the English replied with 261, a first-innings lead of 139, Bannerman produced a contrastingly sparkling performance in the second innings, thrashing 30 runs in 13 minutes. He hit Test cricket's first "six" – then worth five runs – when Lillywhite was launched "clear out of the ring". However, he edged the first ball he received from Ulyett to slip after aiming a somewhat tentative prod at the Yorkshire fast bowler. According to the *Argus*: "The prevalent opinion was that since the accident in the first match, Ulyett has loomed up as large as Cyclops in

The Australian team that toured England in 1878. Back row (l-r): Fred Spofforth, John Conway (manager), Frank Allan. Centre row (l-r): George Bailey, Tom Horan, Tom Garrett, Dave Gregory (captain), Alec Bannerman, Harry Boyle. Front row (l-r): Charles Bannerman, Billy Murdoch, Jack Blackham.

Bannerman's imagination." The hosts were bowled out for 259, leaving England 121 to win, which they achieved with four wickets left to end the two-match "series" all square.

Australia's win in the inaugural Test aroused terrific excitement throughout the land, leading to their maiden tour to England the following year. Although no match on that tour is regarded as a Test, the Australians played 15 first-class games and caused a huge stir when they beat MCC at Lord's in a single day. Bannerman was the tourists' best batsman, with 566 runs at 20.96 and a top score of 61 against the Players. In those days, sizeable scores were rare on uncovered pitches liable to shooters and oddities of bounce. Bannerman played his third and last Test against England at Melbourne in 1879, a game originally billed as "Gentlemen of England (with Ulyett and Emmett) v The Australian XI". Fred "The Demon" Spofforth took Test cricket's first hat-trick in England's first innings total of 113. Australia replied with 256, Charles Bannerman making 15 and brother Alec top-scoring with 73 on debut. Trailing by 143, England made 160 in their second innings before Australia reached an 18-run target without loss.

Slightly shorter than his famous brother, and not as physically powerful, Alec Bannerman played 28 Tests, scoring 1,108 runs at 23.08. In contrast to Charles he was a dour and defensive batsman with endless patience, which only tested that of the crowd. In the words of a later historian of Australian cricket, A. G. Moyes, "At times, the crowd found him as wearisome to the flesh as fleas in a warm bed." After an excruciating innings at Melbourne in 1890, when Alec went scoreless for 70 minutes, the following ditty appeared in print:

Oh Bannerman
We wish you'd change your manner man
We've paid our humble tanner man
To see a bit of fun
You're a beggar though to stick it
But it ain't our sort of cricket
They haven't hit your wicket
Yet you haven't made a run

Whereas Alec's career flourished in the 1880s, Charles's fell away amid mysterious ill health. For several seasons it was said that he was chronically ill without any cause actually being given. Cryptic comments appeared in the press as he was described as "not being for some time past in good health" and "only the ghost of himself now". The *Sydney Mail* wrote that "continued ill health, with no prospect of improvement, compelled him to withdraw from the Australian team" that toured England in 1880. Bannerman's biographer, Alfred James, believes that he might have been "afflicted with some form of mental instability, a breakdown or a reversal of confidence". He added: "There is no evidence that he received treatment privately or in an institution for his mysterious malady." Bannerman effectively had five seasons of illness from 1879-80 to 1883-84 and then suddenly recovered, playing first-class cricket until 1888 and living for almost another 50 years. After Bannerman's death in 1930, William Cooper, a former team-mate, was asked by a journalist what had caused his problems. He answered: "Like a good many other cricketers, success proved to be his failure. He did not and would not remember that he could not 'burn the candle at both ends' and still keep up his form and his reputation. Drink and gambling, it is reputed, was his downfall… It is a question I wish you had not asked for I believe in letting the dead bury their dead."

Marital problems might have been a factor. Bannerman was often absent from his wife, Ellen, through cricket, spending the best part of 14 months away, for example, when the Australians visited England, America and Canada in the late 1870s – a schedule in stark contrast to the modern trend for whirlwind tours when players are often joined by their families. Indeed, Bannerman's recovery seems to have stemmed from the time that he met Mary Ann King, with whom he had an affair and two children in the 1880s. Bannerman eventually left Ellen and their three children to be with a woman ten years his junior. On occasions, as he struggled to finance two households simultaneously, Bannerman appeared in court to answer charges of wife desertion. He only had irregular employment outside of cricket – he worked briefly as a bookmaker – and played as a professional long before a professional structure existed in Australia. Such were his financial woes, the *Sydney Mail* printed this poignant exchange in 1891 under the heading "A Cricketer in Low Circumstances":

> *Judge: Your family is in destitute circumstances. How do you get your living?*
> *Bannerman: By cricketing, your Worship.*
> *Judge: But it's the off season now, and there's not much doing in that line.*
> *Bannerman: I've nothing to say against my wife, your Worship, at all. If you will give me a week to try and get the money, I might get some of it.*

Ellen Bannerman died from cirrhosis of the liver in 1895, aged 44. She'd been suffering "for a few years" from a condition connected with alcoholism. Charles married Mary Ann King in 1900 and stayed heavily involved in cricket, which helped to keep him financially afloat. He coached in Queensland, New Zealand and Sydney and he also umpired 59 first-class matches, including 12 Tests. In retirement, Bannerman attended all the major games at Sydney Cricket Ground, watching from the ground floor of the members' stand. He loved to reminisce with friends and made a point of seeking out promising youngsters to pass on encouragement. Whatever his personal challenges, he was a popular and gregarious man, widely admired and deeply respected.

That respect owed much to his century in the inaugural Test, the highlight of his cricketing life. It was his only first-class hundred to go with nine fifties in a career in which he averaged 21.62; his next-highest score was 83. Bannerman is overwhelmingly remembered for one innings but he was Australia's best batsman between 1875 and 1878, the first in a studded line that continued through the likes of Victor Trumper and Don Bradman. In 1921, Jack Blackham insisted that his old team-mate "never had an equal", asserting that "not even Trumper, Giffen, Hill, Darling, Graham or Gregory ever quite reached Bannerman's standard".

One man who did reach it, of course, and then went well past it, was Bradman, cricket's greatest batsman. Bannerman often watched him playing for New South Wales and, in 1930, seven months before he died on the day that Bradman's double-hundred at The Oval helped Australia regain the Ashes, he saw him score a first-class record 452 not out against Queensland at Sydney. Afterwards, a photograph of the two men was taken beside the members' stand.

Bannerman gives his seal of approval to Don Bradman after the young man's then first-class record 452 not out for New South Wales against Queensland at Sydney in 1930.

Bannerman, wearing an overcoat and a hat, is pictured lightly laying a hand on Bradman's shoulder, like a prophet anointing the chosen one. The old man is clutching a walking stick and a cigarette, while a smiling Bradman faces him in whites. In a subsequent interview, Bannerman announced: "This boy will clip all the records. He is something unusual. He is the sort of batsman you don't see very often. Take my word for it... this young Bradman will break all the records that are breakable."

Records are one thing, firsts another. One distinction that Bradman could never have was that of scoring Test cricket's first hundred. Bannerman's achievement will echo forever. He set the bar for others to raise.

Australia v England

Played at Melbourne Cricket Ground on 15, 16, 17, 19 March, 1877.

Toss: Australia. Result: Australia won by 45 runs.

AUSTRALIA

C. Bannerman retired hurt	165	– b Ulyett	4
N. F. D. Thomson b Hill	1	– c Emmett b Shaw	7
T. P. Horan c Hill b Shaw	12	– c Selby b Hill	20
*D. W. Gregory run out (Jupp)	1	– (9) b Shaw	3
B. B. Cooper b Southerton	15	– b Shaw	3
W. E. Midwinter c Ulyett b Southerton	5	– c Southerton b Ulyett	17
E. J. Gregory c Greenwood b Lillywhite	0	– c Emmett b Ulyett	11
†J. M. Blackham b Southerton	17	– lbw b Shaw	6
T. W. Garrett not out	18	– (4) c Emmett b Shaw	0
T. K. Kendall c Southerton b Shaw	3	– not out	17
J. R. Hodges b Shaw	0	– b Lillywhite	8
B 4, lb 2, w 2	8	B 5, lb 3	8

1/2 (2) 2/40 (3) 3/41 (4)   (169.3 overs) 245
4/118 (5) 5/142 (6) 6/143 (7)
7/197 (8) 8/243 (10) 9/245 (11)

1/7 (1) 2/27 (2)   (68 overs) 104
3/31 (4) 4/31 (3)
5/35 (5) 6/58 (7) 7/71 (8)
8/75 (6) 9/75 (9) 10/104 (11)

In the first innings Bannerman retired hurt at 240-7.

Shaw 55.3–34–51–3; Hill 23–10–42–1; Ulyett 25–12–36–0; Southerton 37–17–61–3; Armitage 3–0–15–0; Lillywhite 14.5–5–19–1; Emmett 12–7–13–0. *Second innings—* Shaw 34–16–38–5; Ulyett 19–7–39–3; Hill 14–6–18–1; Lillywhite 1–0–1–1.

ENGLAND

H. Jupp lbw b Garrett	63	– (3) lbw b Midwinter	4
†J. Selby c Cooper b Hodges	7	– (5) c Horan b Hodges	38
H. R. J. Charlwood c Blackham b Midwinter	36	– (4) b Kendall	13
G. Ulyett lbw b Thomson	10	– (6) b Kendall	24
A. Greenwood c E. J. Gregory b Midwinter	1	– (2) c Midwinter b Kendall	5
T. Armitage c Blackham b Midwinter	9	– (8) b Blackham b Kendall	3
A. Shaw b Midwinter	10	– st Blackham b Kendall	2
T. Emmett b Midwinter	8	– (9) b Kendall	9
A. Hill not out	35	– (1) c Thomson b Kendall	0
*J. Lillywhite c and b Kendall	10	– b Hodges	4
J. Southerton c Cooper b Garrett	6	– not out	1
Lb 1	1	B 4, lb 1	5

1/23 (2) 2/79 (3) 3/98 (4)   (136.1 overs) 196
4/109 (5) 5/121 (6) 6/135 (7)
7/145 (1) 8/145 (8) 9/168 (10) 10/196 (11)

1/0 (1) 2/7 (2)   (66.1 overs) 108
3/20 (3) 4/22 (4)
5/62 (6) 6/68 (7) 7/92 (5)
8/93 (8) 9/100 (10) 10/108 (9)

Hodges 9–0–27–1; Garrett 18.1–10–22–2; Kendall 38–16–54–1; Midwinter 54–23–78–5; Thomson 17–10–14–1. *Second innings—* Kendall 33.1–12–55–7; Midwinter 19–7–23–1; D. W. Gregory 5–1–9–0; Garrett 2–0–9–0; Hodges 7–5–7–2.

Umpires: C. A. Reid and R. B. Terry.

2

Billy Murdoch (211)
Australia versus England
The Oval 1884

If Australia's leading fast bowler of the 19th century had got his way, the man who broke Charles Bannerman's record would have played in the inaugural Test. Fred "The Demon" Spofforth had wanted his New South Wales team-mate Billy Murdoch to keep wicket instead of Victoria's Jack Blackham, prompting Spofforth's withdrawal. In a letter to Dave Gregory, the Australian captain and New South Wales selector, Spofforth fumed: "I notice that in the selection of the team you have left Murdoch out; so you might just as well draw a pen through my name, as it would be no use my playing without I had someone that could take my bowling behind the wicket, which I am sure Blackham cannot... If you think that it is the best team that can be got, all right; but I don't think it is... So I beg to withdraw my name from the number, as I cannot stand Melbourne doing all the work. Yours, etc. Fred R. Spofforth." Spofforth's stance was heavily criticised, the Melbourne papers perceiving it as arrogance. *The Australasian* said that the Sydney man refused to play unless "his own special wicketkeeper" was chosen, sarcastically adding that "as this could not be arranged, this modest gentleman had to be left behind". Ironically, Blackham would go on to become one of the greatest cricketers of the day, earning the nickname "The Prince of Wicketkeepers".

Spofforth's loyalty stemmed not only from the fact that he and Murdoch were team-mates, but also that they were close friends who'd grown up together. Like Charles Bannerman's family, Murdoch's had moved to Sydney when he was a boy; in their case, some 550 miles from Sandhurst (later Bendigo) in Victoria. Murdoch and Spofforth played cricket in the Balmain suburb of Sydney along with Murdoch's older brother, Gilbert, practising on a rough dirt pitch from dawn until dusk. Murdoch and Spofforth remained as thick as thieves through the Albert Cricket Club in Sydney and into the New South Wales first team, where they formed a prodigious partnership. After Australia's victory in the inaugural Test, both men played in what came to be known as the second Test. Picked as a specialist batsman, with Blackham once more keeping wicket, Murdoch scored three and eight as England won the so-called "Return Combination Match". However, he took the gloves on the final day when Blackham had sunstroke, and it was mainly as a wicketkeeper/batsman that he was chosen for the tour to England the following year as Blackham's deputy. Before long, though, even "The Demon" was forced to concede that Blackham was a demon behind the stumps, with Murdoch making his name as a batsman.

Murdoch shot to prominence in 1880, scoring a century in the first Test match played in England. After W. G. Grace hit 152 in England's first innings at The Oval, Murdoch – by then Australia's captain – bet him a sovereign that he would beat his score. He struck 153 not out in the second innings but ran out of partners as the tourists lost by five wickets.

That was the closest that anyone had come to beating Bannerman's record before Murdoch himself did so. The one-off 1880 Test was shoved into the schedule as an early-September afterthought, with most counties having shunned the Australians. This stemmed from a serious incident involving Murdoch the previous winter when Lord Harris's England side played New South Wales. All hell broke loose when Murdoch was given run out by umpire George Coulthard, a Victorian whose impartiality was doubted by the Sydney crowd. Lord Harris, in trying to protect the umpire from the advancing hordes, was struck with a whip or a stick. The high-handed Harris, one of the most influential figures of the time, followed up with some inflammatory remarks in the press about Australia's lack of sportsmanship, souring relations between the countries and casting a long shadow over the 1880 tour. However, Murdoch and his men had a strong ally in W. G. Grace, who recognised that there were sovereigns aplenty to be made from a fixture between the tourists and a representative England team. Consequently, Grace persuaded Harris to relax his stance and lead England at The Oval, Harris shaking hands with Murdoch before the game in a public gesture of peace.

Two years later, in the corresponding Test at the same ground, Murdoch was involved in an even more controversial run-out that inadvertently gave birth to the Ashes. In Australia's second innings, he turned a ball from Lancashire all-rounder Allan Steel into the leg side for a single. Although Sammy Jones, his batting partner, comfortably made his ground, Jones was run out by Grace when he left his crease to pat down a divot, assuming that the ball was dead. The Australians were incensed, Spofforth calling Grace a cheat and insisting: "This will lose you the match." True to his

Lord Harris, one of game's most powerful figures in the late 19ᵗʰ and early 20ᵗʰ century.

word, Spofforth – 6ft 3ins of bristling aggression, with piercing eyes and eagle nose – took seven wickets as England were routed for 77 in pursuit of 85. Amid the suffocating drama, *Wisden* reported that "one spectator dropped dead from excitement, and another unconsciously gnawed away the handle of his umbrella". For the first time, Australia had beaten England in their own backyard, prompting the mock obituary in the *Sporting Times* that bemoaned the death of English cricket, whose "body will be cremated and the ashes taken to Australia". The following winter, Murdoch lost the Ashes when Australia slipped to a 2–1 defeat. The Ashes also remained in England in 1884, when Murdoch made his fourth visit, his third as captain, and when he broke Bannerman's record for the highest Test score.

After Australia had the best of a weather-ruined First Test in Manchester, they lost the Second at Lord's by an innings. They dominated the drawn finale at The Oval, where Murdoch recorded Test cricket's first double-hundred. It was an unusually high-scoring match in a low-scoring era, helped by an August heatwave that deadened the pitch. According to the *Melbourne Argus*, the opening day was "remarkably hot" and "one of the most trying days that has been experienced in London for a number of years". It was the archetypal batting day, and "a shade of disappointment was noticeable on the countenances of many an Englishman when the news went round that Lord Harris had lost the toss". The stifling conditions did not deter a crowd of around 18,000, who placed "handkerchiefs or newspapers over their heads as protection from the sun" and used "palm-leaf fans to keep themselves cool".

On a pitch "as hard as asphalt pavement", with the outfield "as firm as a billiard table", Alec Bannerman was an early casualty, popping a ball from Yorkshire left-arm spinner Ted Peate into the hands of point. "This was certainly a poor beginning," lamented the *Melbourne Argus*, "and Australian supporters looked gloomy as Murdoch, the next defender, left the pavilion." Despite the heat, which reached 94 in the shade, England bowled well in the early stages. Murdoch and opening batsman Percy McDonnell were challenged by Peate and his Yorkshire team-mate George Ulyett, one of three survivors from the inaugural Test along with Australia's Billy Midwinter and Jack Blackham. Murdoch got his arms moving by cutting Ulyett to the boundary, thereby executing his favourite shot. "The sweetest stroke of the whole game is, without doubt, the cut," he announced in an instruction book in 1902. Murdoch unfurled a few more en route to 36 at lunch, which Australia took at 130 for one (McDonnell 86). Afterwards, McDonnell, a brilliant attacking player nicknamed "Greatheart", was caught at slip by Peate off Ulyett for 103, having shared with his captain 143 in a dazzling display. Murdoch was now assisted by Henry "Tup" Scott, a 25-year-old Victorian right-hander whose batting, said one writer, was "noted for grit rather than gaiety". Scott, who acquired the nickname "Tup" due to his love of London's tuppence bus rides, was more gay than gritty this time, imposing himself on a wilting attack. Murdoch, some two months short of his 30th birthday, batted at his own unhurried pace, leading the fielders a merry dance.

Of medium height and robust frame, with a wide and immaculately groomed moustache, Murdoch was built in the mould of Charles Bannerman. He was fast on his feet and renowned for his coolness under pressure. Warm and

Billy Murdoch in his stance.

friendly, with keen brown eyes, he invariably looked on the bright side of life. He often smiled when batting and emitted a comic snort if a ball misbehaved. Murdoch was also renowned for a singular leg-side shot in which he lifted his left front leg and played the ball away beneath it, something not dissimilar to that developed by Nat Sciver, the England women's cricketer, in 2017, popularly known as the 'Nat-Meg'. *Wisden* felt that Murdoch "needed sunshine and a lively pitch to be at his best" and "did not rise to great heights on wickets spoiled by rain". The Almanack added that "daring hooks and pulls" were "not within his range". However, it stressed that "few batsmen have been better worth looking at, his style leaving no loophole for criticism".

At the ground where he'd scored his first Test century, Murdoch reached his second – and last – at ten-to-five with a leg-side four off the Nottinghamshire batsman William Scotton. The 20 balls delivered by Scotton were the only ones of his Test career, with all 11 players bowling in a Test innings for the first time. Even the Honourable Alfred Lyttelton, the Middlesex wicketkeeper and the first man to play cricket and football for England, tried medium-pace as the main cast rested. *Bell's Life* described Lyttelton's offerings as "very erratic" with the ball "generally going wide on the leg side". At stumps, Murdoch had 145, Scott 101, and Australia were sitting pretty on 363 for two. Murdoch had offered one chance; he was dropped on 46 by keeper Lyttelton off Ulyett.

Day two was not so devilishly hot, with a light breeze tempering the strength of the sun. A crowd of around 14,000 saw Scott add one to his overnight score before he was caught behind off Billy Barnes, the Nottinghamshire medium-pace-bowling all-rounder. It ended a stand of 207 with Murdoch, then the highest for any Test wicket. In the previous Test at Lord's, Murdoch had caught Scott while fielding as a substitute for England's W. G. Grace, an unthinkable concept nowadays. With Test cricket still to be officially recognised (it was another decade from enjoying that status), there was no sense of drama as Murdoch approached and passed Bannerman's score. Newspapers didn't mention the fact, and there was no suggestion that the crowd acknowledged it in any way. Murdoch had a second life on 171 when he was badly missed by Lancashire batsman Dick Barlow at slip off Ulyett, whose piqued reaction belied his nickname "Happy Jack". In a sketch of the match, *The Illustrated Sporting and Dramatic News* gave a running description of Barlow's blunder:

> *"The sun is dead in his eyes, and he has closed his hands a thought too speedily, and has received the impact of the ball on his knuckles. From an object of derision he is transformed into one of pity when it is seen that his hand is cut. Grace comes to the fore in a new capacity in the cricket field, and gravely proceeds to bandage the injured member secundum artem, an operation watched with intense interest. How he must rejoice over such an opportunity of occasionally practising his other profession."*

After cutting Barnes for four to bring up his double-hundred straight after lunch, Murdoch was dropped for a third time off Ulyett on 205. By now, "Happy Jack" was most definitely "Unhappy Jack", although the chance to Steel at mid-on was by no means easy. Murdoch was eventually out for 211, caught by Peate at slip off Barnes, and retired to "loud and prolonged applause in which Englishmen joined". He'd batted for eight hours, ten minutes and struck 24 fours, nine threes, 22 twos and 44 singles. Appraising his efforts, *The Australasian* said: "He was almost painfully careful at first, but his batting never degenerated into a niggling and blocking style of play, and whenever a really loose ball presented itself, he made full use of the opportunity – in other words, his innings was that of a great batsman. From first to last he took no liberties, and showed no mercy." *The Times* called it "a splendid innings, but not so good as his 153 in 1880, as he gave three chances, and the fierce hitting of McDonnell had knocked a lot of sting out of the English bowling".

Murdoch's departure left Australia 494 for six, with all-rounder George Giffen and hard-hitting batsman George Bonnor having also departed. The three-day game was now past its halfway stage, but the Australians had no choice but to continue batting as declarations were not allowed until 1889. It needed the reintroduction of wicketkeeper Lyttelton to send them packing. This time, bowling in his pads from the Vauxhall End, Lyttelton served up underarm lobs while Grace kept wicket – a tactic of "comic desperation", thought *The Australasian*. From his first delivery, Lyttelton had Midwinter caught down the leg side by Grace, who returned the gloves to him when the bowling resumed at the opposite end. Lyttelton followed that by trapping Blackham lbw, bowling Spofforth and having last man Harry Boyle caught by Harris at mid-on. In an eye-blink, he'd taken four for eight in an incredible spell, the only wickets of his first-class career. Australia were all out for 551, beating the previous highest Test score of 420 by England in the 1880 game.

When the hosts replied, Grace looked a good bet to answer Murdoch's double-hundred with a sizeable innings of his own. He hit Bonnor for three leg-side boundaries in quick

The Australians in 1884. Standing (l-r): Jack Blackham, Henry "Tup" Scott, George Alexander (manager), Billy Midwinter, Percy McDonnell, William Cooper. Sitting (l-r): George Giffen, Harry Boyle, Billy Murdoch (captain), George Bonnor, Joey Palmer. In front (l-r): Alec Bannerman, Fred Spofforth.

succession to bring the crowd to its feet. However, when he reached 19 and the score was 32, England's champion ran himself out. Initially, Grace stood his ground, which only whipped up the crowd, who turned their ire on umpire Charles Pullin. In echoes of the Sydney riot of 1879, when the crowd vented their anger at Murdoch's run-out against Lord Harris's men, Pullin needed a police escort back to the pavilion as hundreds remonstrated at the close of play. After their own countrymen had been at fault for the Sydney rumpus, the Australian press seized this chance to lampoon the English. The *Melbourne Argus* said "the Surrey mob certainly acted up to their reputation for being the most ruffianly in England" and that "verily the Sydney larrikin is a polished gentleman compared to the Surrey rough". The *Adelaide Observer* chimed in: "There are a few people who seem to attend the matches solely for the purpose of creating rows if they can, and these are making Kennington Oval an evil reputation."

Play was further delayed when spectators encroached on the outfield in the days when they could sit and watch beside the boundary. Giffen, in trying to stop one ball, ran into a group of them some 15 yards inside the rope. When Giffen raised his arms in protest, Lord Harris stormed down from the pavilion and warned the offenders: "If you don't give the Australians fair play, I will give them the match." As it was, the game petered out as England replied with 346, the great Surrey batsman Walter Read scoring a match-saving hundred from No. 10, a riotous innings that betrayed his indignation at having to bat so low in the order. Following on, England reached 85 for two in the little time left, the *Sunday Times* insisting that they won the series 1–0 under "false pretences" as Australia had the better of two of the three Tests.

No comment exists from Murdoch on his innings at a time when newspapers rarely interviewed players. Indeed, he is the only record-holder whose observations are not recorded. Remarkably, it has been possible even to trace some reflections from Charles Bannerman on his 165. Interviewed by *The Recorder*, South Australia, one month before his 70th birthday, Bannerman was asked what he remembered of the famous game and began by referencing Murdoch's omission:

> "We had a good side, but it was properly thought that the venture was rather too bold, and our chances were not improved when Spofforth declined to play if Murdoch was not chosen as wicketkeeper. He told Dave Gregory, who was sole selector for New South Wales, that Murdoch was the only keeper who could take his bowling. Blackham was picked in his place. Seems funny, doesn't it, that he should have objected to the man who was to leave his mark as the prince of wicketkeepers? Anyway, we played without 'Spoff', and won by 45."

> "Thanks to your great innings," the reporter reminded him.

> "Don't make much of what I did. Don't forget Tom Kendall's bowling. What a pity he didn't go to England with us in '78. He was a left-hander, and one of the very best."

> Recalling his hundred, Bannerman said: "I picked my ball and made most of my runs in front of the wicket. I never used the back-cut, because there were so many men behind the wicket, and it was so easy to make a mistake. My favourite stroke was between the mid-off and cover, and I could push them away to the on as well.

*Did I pull like the modern batsman? Of course, when
I got the right ball."*

Bannerman remembered the injury that forced him
to retire hurt – "the nail was smashed and the finger
so badly split that it was put in splints". He was asked,
in conclusion, what the bowling was like.

*"Well, I reckon that the English team was one of the
strongest in bowling that ever came out. It included
Alfred Shaw, the most perfect length bowler England has
had; Jim Lillywhite, who was steady and accurate; Tom
Emmett, a fine left-hander; Allen Hill, who was very
fast; George Ulyett, not nearly so fast as Hill but a real
good 'un; Armitage, who bowled slows, and Southerton,
a fine medium-pace bowler. I tell you that the English
attack had plenty of variety, and it was quality right
through."*

After ending his record-breaking 1884 tour by leading the
Non-Smokers to a nine-wicket victory at Lord's against a
Smokers' team that included Fred Spofforth, Murdoch
returned to Australia. It was a fortuitous voyage to say the
least; he met and fell in love with Jemima Watson, the
daughter of a Scottish-born Australian gold-mining magnate,
which was good news in more ways than one as Murdoch
had been declared bankrupt at the start of the decade after an
ill-judged shipping investment. Following a brief romance,
they married four days before the first Test of the return
series against England at Adelaide in 1884. This match led to
a great schism in Australian cricket and saw Murdoch quit
the sport for over five years.

At the time, the accepted convention was that the larger expenses incurred by a touring team entitled them to a larger share of gate receipts. Murdoch disagreed and demanded that the Australians received 50% of gate receipts for the Second Test in Melbourne. The English contingent, led by the Nottinghamshire pair of Alfred Shaw and Arthur Shrewsbury, considered this unfair since the Australians were amateurs and playing at home. They felt that 30% was the most they could give and that the Australians were being distinctly ungenerous. Most of the Australian press and public agreed and accused Murdoch and co of penny-pinching. Spofforth, in fact, was one of the loudest voices against the ensuing player strike, which saw an entirely different Australian team at the MCG. Although some striking players returned later in the series, Murdoch refused to budge and argued that as his side had raised cricket's profile and profitability, they should be properly compensated. What sympathy there was grew thin, however, as Australia fell to a 3-2 defeat. One newspaper advised Murdoch to "give the gate-money racket a rest", while *Wisden* accused him and his players of "unpatriotic conduct".

A sensitive soul beneath the ebullient exterior, Murdoch took the criticism to heart and turned to his second profession – law. A graduate of Sydney University, he was a qualified solicitor who'd set up practice after the 1880 tour to England in Cootamundra, New

A vintage illustration of Murdoch from the contemporary journal Sporting Mirror.

South Wales, where Don Bradman was born almost three decades later. Murdoch dealt with such matters as master-and-servant rights, sheep-stealing and breaches of contract and practised whenever his cricket permitted. His legal experience gave him a lucid grasp of the technicalities involved in cricket pay disputes, while his marriage to the daughter of one of the country's richest men meant that he could afford to stand firm on points of principle.

In late 1885, one year after the row, Billy and Jemima Murdoch moved to Melbourne, where he was admitted into the Victorian Supreme Court. While in Melbourne he rejected entreaties to end his cricketing exile by playing for Victoria, against whom he'd struck his career-best score some three years earlier. Murdoch's 321 for New South Wales was the first triple-hundred in Australia and the second-highest score in first-class cricket at the time behind W. G. Grace's 344 for Gentlemen of MCC versus Kent at Canterbury in 1876. Murdoch missed the fourth day of the match due to a court engagement in Cootamundra but caught a morning milk train back to the ground in time for the start of day five as his side completed an innings win.

Without Murdoch, their leader and linchpin, Australia struggled in the latter part of the 1880s. He missed 13 Tests, ten of which were lost, and another two tours to England. In 1890, with Australia's great days under his captaincy a fading memory, Murdoch was finally persuaded to return, aged, 35 to lead a tour to Grace's England. But the hosts won the three-match series 2–0 as Murdoch lost his third Ashes campaign as captain, a fate not suffered by an Australian until Ricky Ponting over 100 years later. Despite it all, Murdoch remained popular with English crowds, and he himself had a

soft spot for England. After the 1890 tour he settled there
with Jemima and their children, making one last Test
appearance for England, in fact, against South Africa at Cape
Town in 1892. Murdoch scored 12 in an innings win and kept
wicket in South Africa's second innings; he is one of only 15
men to have played Test cricket for two different countries.

From 1893 to 1899, he captained Sussex, taking them from
also-rans to their then-highest finish of fifth in his final season
in charge. He inspired great devotion from his players, who
responded to his unfailingly positive attitude. The *Adelaide
Observer* wrote: "He had the faculty, invaluable in a captain, of
being able to inspire confidence in his men. No task was ever
permitted by him to be insuperable. 'Impossible' was a word
scored out of his vocabulary." Murdoch also had a great liking
for cricket's social side, another fact appreciated by colleagues.
Some critics felt that he carried this fancy a little too far, the
cricket historian Sir Home Gordon describing him as "a genial
man with much appreciation of other players", but with "too
little control of his own inclinations". Murdoch's taste for a
good time was highlighted when Australia lost the 1882-83
Ashes to Ivo Bligh's tourists. Summing up the series, *The
Australasian* declared: "The captain was perhaps the greatest
disappointment. Instead of showing his companions a good
example and endeavouring to keep them up to their proper
standard, he seemed to prefer shooting, picnics and social
parties, which might have been left until the team disbanded.
Picnics and champagne are not conducive to good cricket."

Murdoch's larger-than-life personality certainly appealed
to Grace, with whom he had a lasting friendship. After
relinquishing the Sussex captaincy, Murdoch joined Grace's
London County, a short-lived club that played first-class
games from 1900 to 1904. The friends had much in

"Father" and "Muvver": W. G. Grace and Murdoch at Sheffield Park, Sussex.

common – boundless charisma, a shared sense of fun and a sharp eye for cricket's financial possibilities. They also dwelt on the same high plane, with Murdoch effectively Australia's WG – albeit the first to acknowledge Grace's pre-eminence. At London County they were nicknamed "Father" and "Muvver", their friendship setting a happy tone. They pulled each other's legs constantly and were relentlessly competitive, whether playing cricket or other sports. Once, at a game in Wiltshire, Grace bet Murdoch that he could catch more fish in the river near to where they were staying than Murdoch could score runs in the match, echoing their wager in the 1880 Test when Murdoch pocketed Grace's sovereign. To make sure of victory this time, Grace got up at four in the morning and caught 100 fish, only for Murdoch to score 103. Grace also remembered a golfing story that captured their bond.

> *"We were digging our way round when Murdoch drove into a deep sand bunker rather at the side of the course. A few spectators were with us, but when Billy got into the bunker he was hidden from view. We saw the ball come out amid the usual shower of sand, and everyone cried, 'Well out, good shot.' At lunch one of the members remarked on Billy's excellent recovery, saying he'd soon be a plus man at that rate, when Billy, having taken it all in quite seriously, whispered to me, 'Knew I should never get out of the blessed hole, so I took a double handful of sand and the ball and flung 'em out.'"*

Murdoch's humour also made a strong impression on his Sussex team-mate C. B. Fry, who admired the way he "always thought he was going to make a century… no matter whether he had a month of minute scores behind him". Fry sketched his friend vividly. "He does not commit puns nor splutter epigrams; he is simply, genuinely and unaffectedly amusing. Instead of 'It will rain hard today,' he says, 'Boys, the sparrows will be washed out.' Instead of 'I'm in good form,' he asks in a concentrated voice, 'Where's Surrey?' But it's the way, not the words." Fry, who described Murdoch as "the best possible pal before, during and after a match, wet or fine, sparrows or no sparrows", remembered the "cheerful, well-fed voice", the "tanned face" and "neat black moustache brimming with vitality". He added: "His spirit would refuse to be unfortunate, his body scorn incapacity for meat and drink. No wonder he led the Australians well in the old days – a fit Odysseus to meet our mighty bearded Ajax."

Murdoch's 211 remained the highest Test score by an Australian until January 1911, when Victor Trumper scored an unbeaten 214 against South Africa at Adelaide. Murdoch was in Australia at the time having returned briefly with Jemima to attend to the disposal of her father's estate. Murdoch went alone to the next Test in Melbourne and was talking with an old friend during the lunch break when he suddenly let out a sharp cry and slumped on a table in front of him. As concern engulfed him, he explained that it was a recurring attack of neuralgia and that there was nothing to worry about. Moments later, he suffered a stroke and collapsed to the ground, falling into a coma. Although four doctors in the pavilion tried to ease the pressure on his brain by opening a vein in his wrist, it was too late. Murdoch, the "fit Odysseus" of C. B. Fry's fond reminiscence, died a short time later, aged 56. As the tragic news spread, the flag at the MCG was lowered to half-mast and the players wore black armbands.

Murdoch's body was shipped back to England, his funeral held at London's Kensal Green cemetery in May. As a mark of respect, play at all county grounds was briefly suspended. Amid the tributes in the London press, with *The Times* describing him as "the first great Colonial batsman" as Charles Bannerman's career was "too short to qualify him to be put on the same pedestal", the comments of one former comrade stood out. Fred "The Demon" Spofforth, who'd grown up with Murdoch and shared so many happy times with him – not least the win over England that gave birth to the Ashes – delivered a heartfelt reaction to his old friend's death. Spofforth, who'd also settled in England after joining Derbyshire CCC, said simply: "Billy was at his greatest at the Oval in 1884, when he scored 211. As a captain, he knew how to instruct, and when to take off a bowler, and he had the gift of inspiring confidence in his team."

England v Australia

Played at Kennington Oval, London, on 11, 12, 13 August, 1884.

Toss: Australia. Result: Match drawn.

AUSTRALIA

A. C. Bannerman c Read b Peate	4	F. R. Spofforth b Lyttelton	4
P. S. McDonnell c Ulyett b Peate	103	H. F. Boyle c Harris b Lyttelton	1
*W. L. Murdoch c Peate b Barnes	211		
H. J. H. Scott c Lyttelton b Barnes	102	B 7, lb 10	17
G. Giffen c Steel b Ulyett	32		
G. J. Bonnor c Read b Grace	8	1/15 (1) 2/158 (2) (311 overs) 551	
W. E. Midwinter c †Grace b Lyttelton	30	3/365 (4) 4/432 (5)	
†J. M. Blackham lbw b Lyttelton	31	5/454 (6) 6/494 (3) 7/532 (7)	
G. E. Palmer not out	8	8/545 (8) 9/549 (10) 10/551 (11)	

Peate 63–25–99–2; Ulyett 56–24–96–1; Steel 34–7–71–0; Barnes 52–25–81–2; Barlow 50–22–72–0; Grace 24–14–23–1; Read 7–0–36–0; Scotton 5–1–20–0; Harris 5–1–15–0; Lyttelton 12–5–19–4; Shrewsbury 3–2–2–0.

ENGLAND

W. G. Grace run out (Bannerman)	19		
W. H. Scotton c Scott b Giffen	90		
W. Barnes c Midwinter b Spofforth	19		
A. Shrewsbury c Blackham b Midwinter	10 –	(3) c Scott b Giffen	37
A. G. Steel lbw b Palmer	31		
G. Ulyett c Bannerman b Palmer	10		
R. G. Barlow c Murdoch b Palmer	0 –	(1) not out	21
*Lord Harris lbw b Palmer	14 –	(4) not out	6
†A. Lyttelton b Spofforth	8 –	(2) b Boyle	17
W. W. Read b Boyle	117		
E. Peate not out	4		
B 8, lb 7, w 6, nb 3	24	B 3, lb 1	4

1/32 (1) 2/60 (3) 3/75 (4)   (198 overs) 346   1/22 (2)   (2 wkts, 26 overs) 85
4/120 (5) 5/136 (6) 6/136 (7)   2/73 (3)
7/160 (8) 8/181 (9) 9/332 (2) 10/346 (10)

Bonnor 13–4–33–0; Palmer 54–19–90–4; Spofforth 58–31–81–2; Boyle 13–7–24–1; Midwinter 31–16–41–1; Giffen 26–13–36–1; Scott 3–0–17–0. *Second innings* – Spofforth 6–2–14–0; Boyle 8–1–32–1; Giffen 7–1–18–1; Midwinter 3–0–15–0; Palmer 2–1–2–0.

Umpires: F. H. Farrands and C. K. Pullin.

3

"Tip" Foster (287)
England versus Australia
Sydney 1903

It is the archetypal quiz question: name the only man to have captained England at cricket and football? Answer: R. E. Foster, known as "Tip".

Reginald Erskine Foster, to give him his full name, was one of England's leading amateurs. He got the nickname "Tip" while studying at Oxford due to his "tip-and-run" style of batting. Foster captained England in three of his eight Test matches and led England's footballers in the last of his six internationals playing at inside-forward. Two years before breaking Billy Murdoch's record for the highest Test score, Foster played in England's first football match against Germany, scoring six times in a 12–0 win at White Hart Lane. At Oxford, from where he graduated to a parallel career on the Stock Exchange, Foster gained Blues in cricket, football, golf and racquets. If there was a ball or bat involved, "Tip" was in his element.

He came from a celebrated cricketing family, one of seven brothers to play for Worcestershire. They were cricket's answer to the Seven Sisters, and "Tip" was easily the brightest star. Starting with the eldest, the brothers Foster were Harry, Wilfrid, "Tip", Basil, Geoffrey, Maurice and Neville. As a result, Worcestershire were nicknamed

"Fostershire", with "Tip", Harry and Maurice all captaining the club. Harry made the most appearances, scored the most runs and led the side the longest. "Tip" was the only one who played for England, while the others had fairly modest careers. Basil, who played 34 first-class games, enjoyed greater success as an actor. He appeared several times on the London stage and later took up theatrical management.

Although one of the finest batsmen of the Golden Age, Foster's selection for the 1903-04 Ashes tour was criticised. He was uncapped and only played intermittently due to stockbroking work; Foster, in fact, had one full season (1901) and played just 139 first-class matches. He'd appeared only three times during the 1903 English summer and ten times the previous year, managing one hundred in that time. But his success in 1901, when he'd scored over 2,000 runs and averaged over 50, marked him down as a special talent – as did his then-record 171 in the previous season's Varsity match, plus a century in each innings for the Gentlemen against the Players, making him the first to achieve that feat. Foster's maiden hundred had come against Hampshire at Worcester in 1899 when he scored a century in each innings along with brother

"Tip" Foster, whose selection for the 1903-04 Ashes tour was criticised.

Wilfrid. It was the first instance of two brothers scoring twin hundreds in a first-class match. Although Foster's aesthetic style was never in doubt, some feared he was not solid enough to flourish Down Under. Archie MacLaren, to whom *Wisden* compared him in the pantheon of Golden Age batsmen, wrote before the tour that Foster, 25, was "not the type of batsman to succeed in Australia, where matches are won by steadiness rather than brilliancy".

MacLaren, the Lancashire captain, was an influential voice having led England in their previous 14 Tests, half of which they'd lost. He was overlooked as captain for the 1903-04 tour in preference to Middlesex batsman Plum Warner, a decision criticised even more than Foster's selection. Warner, 29, who would manage England during the Bodyline series, was not even captain of his county side. He rather fell into the England job after Stanley Jackson, the stylish Yorkshire all-rounder, turned it down due to "business, military and domestic commitments", insisting that he could not drop all to go on a long tour. MacLaren, 31, had no desire to play under a junior man and he also had a frosty relationship with Lord Hawke, the Yorkshire potentate and MCC chairman of selectors. This was the first England squad chosen and managed by MCC, with all previous England trips to Australia the result of private enterprises. As well as advising England not to pick Foster, MacLaren cautioned against taking Sydney Barnes, the finest bowler available, as he was "temperamentally unsuited to a long tour and almost certain to break down in health". MacLaren had found the famously irascible Barnes difficult to control at Lancashire and on England's previous visit to Australia in 1901-02. So much so, legend has it that when a fierce storm raged on the journey out, MacLaren exclaimed: "If we go down, at least that bugger Barnes will go down with us."

In the absence of such as MacLaren, Jackson and Barnes, Warner's was considered one of the weakest teams to have left England. The Australians were widely expected to win their fifth successive Ashes series, a sequence that began in 1897-98. Foster was one of three amateurs in the squad along with Warner and Middlesex leg-spinner Bernard Bosanquet, the man who invented the googly – aka the "Bosie". Bosanquet's call-up – after a modest career – was also derided and dismissed as favouritism on the part of Warner, his county colleague. However, the professional element of the squad was strong, with such as the Yorkshire all-rounders George Hirst and Wilfred Rhodes, plus two of the finest batsmen of the day in Lancashire's Johnny Tyldesley and Surrey's Tom Hayward. The bowling attack had skill and variety and the side, in general, nothing to lose.

Foster's tour started poorly; he was run out for two in the opening match against South Australia. But he hit 71 in the next match, an innings win against Victoria, and followed up with 35 in another innings win against New South Wales. Warner liked what he saw, writing in his tour diary that Foster was "playing brilliantly and quite up to his form of the English summers of 1900 and 1901". In the final warm-up before the First Test in Sydney, where he took Murdoch's record, Foster scored 105 and 47 against Fifteen of Newcastle and captained England in a two-day draw.

It is unknown whether Warner parroted the modern cliché that "a good start to the Test series is vital", but his side made one after he lost the toss on a perfect pitch. Warner said the surface had "a brown, glazed look as if a hot iron had been passed over it and had scorched the grass". It was faster than the usual Sydney wicket, with the weather just as perfect for a crowd of around 10,000. They were scarcely able to believe their eyes as Australia lost three wickets inside the first 20 minutes – the prized ones, too, of Victor Trumper, Reggie Duff and Clem Hill.

Foster triggered the collapse, brilliantly catching Trumper at slip off his Worcestershire team-mate Ted Arnold's first ball in Test cricket. It was a fast chance to his left and Foster flew through the air to take it one-handed, falling hard on his shoulder and being "loudly cheered for his clever work". Tall and thin, with angular face and natural agility, Foster was one of the best slips in England. "He had enough of the height and all the quickness of instructive movement necessary for the position," said *The Times*. With the first ball of his next over, Arnold, a tall and lithe paceman, had Duff caught behind by Warwickshire's Dick Lilley as he tried to force between cover and point. When Lilley then caught Hill off left-arm pace bowler Hirst, Australia were 12 for three and England's underdogs firmly on top.

Monty Noble, the Australia captain, steadied the ship alongside "The Big Ship", aka Warwick Armstrong, then a slim 24-year-old who became a 22-stone giant – hence the subsequent nickname. They added 106 before Armstrong was Bosanquet's first Test victim, bowled by a "Bosie". "Bosanquet is really valuable," wrote Warner. "He can bowl as badly as anyone in the world, but, when he gets a length, those slow 'googlies', as the Australian papers call them, are apt to paralyse the greatest players. Could he be mechanically certain of his length, I venture to think that he would be the

The England team before the first Test in Sydney. Standing (l-r): Albert Knight (twelfth man), Len Braund, Bernard Bosanquet, Albert Relf, Wilfred Rhodes, Ted Arnold. Sitting (l-r): George Hirst, "Tip" Foster, Plum Warner (captain), Tom Hayward, Dick Lilley, Johnny Tyldesley.

most difficult bowler in the world, for seldom indeed does one find a batsman who can detect that 'off-break with the leg-break action'."

Noble, a batsman of "rare style", thought *Wisden*, added 82 with Bert Hopkins, an attacking player from New South Wales. However, Australia slipped from 200 for four to 285 all out to undo the good work of Noble and co. Noble was ninth out for the top score of 133, his only Test century, brilliantly caught by a diving Foster at square leg off Arnold, England's best bowler with four for 76.

On an overcast second day, Foster began his famous innings midway through the afternoon with the score standing at 73 for three. He'd been due to go in at No. 4 but, with the pitch tricky after overnight rain, Warner held him back and promoted tailender Arnold until conditions improved. So tough were conditions, with Warner falling for a duck and Hayward for 15, that the 53 scored by Tyldesley – whose dismissal brought Foster to the crease – was described by Warner as "perhaps the best innings of his life", a significant comment given that the silky right-hander scored 37,897 first-class runs and 86 hundreds. Without it, England might not have weathered the early threats posed by seamers Frank Laver and Bill Howell, plus left-arm spinner Jack Saunders, which helped Foster to flourish once the pitch had dried. Not that Foster found it easy to start with. He was beaten several times as he played with exaggerated care alongside Arnold, who moved to 27 before being superbly caught by Laver at short leg off Armstrong. According to Warner, Foster was "scarcely at his best" and there were "one or two faulty hits". But he battled through to 30 out of 135 for four at tea, when "the heat was oppressive and the flies a source of worry to the batsmen and fielders".

Batting got easier in the final session, but by no means easy per se. Foster and the cheerful Somerset all-rounder Len Braund were never fluent against probing bowling before a packed and lively Saturday crowd. One short of his fifty, Foster almost gave a catch to Syd Gregory at cover, and there were close shaves at both ends. But the fifth-wicket pair held firm to reduce the deficit to 42 as England reached 243 for four at stumps.

Although Foster had several challenging moments, Warner said that "every now and again he brought off a beautiful off-drive or late cut". Overall, though, he felt Foster's performance "somewhat disappointing, although invaluable to his side". Warner added that "it must be remembered that the ball always required careful watching, and that the bowling was of high quality". The *Sydney Referee* considered Foster's innings "deadly dull for a long time" and said he was "troubled by the bowling". Foster illuminated little of his own thoughts in an unpublished tour diary, his entry for that night reading:

> *"Braund and I kept plugging away and were together at close of play, 73 (self) and 67 (Braund). The attendance was grand being 37,000."*

Sunday was a rest day and Foster jotted:

> *"Went to church. Very hot day. Called on Walter Allen [Gubby Allen's father]."*

When the game resumed on Monday, December 14, 1903, the pitch was again in perfect condition, the weather warm and sunny. There were about 12,000 spectators as Sydney began a new working week. If anything, the pitch had quickened and the ball came on to the bat more readily. This helped Foster to use the pace of it with his naturally strong and supple wrists. "He had glorious wrists and every stroke on the board," said *The Times*, which maintained that "there was no more delightful batsman to watch". Foster, it said, "seemed to be one of those fortunate mortals who could go in and feel that he was likely to get runs".

After being made to scrap for their runs on the Saturday, Foster and Braund now collared the bowling. They had a neck-and-neck race to reach three figures, Foster winning with a late cut for four off Laver – "about the finest stroke of the whole tour", said Warner. Braund, whom his Somerset team-mate R. C. Robertson-Glasgow called "one of the great characters of England", a man who "illustrates a stroke with a casual cane", reached his hundred in the next over. But he was yorked off the next ball he faced for 102, ending a stand with Foster of 192 that left England 309 for five. It was the first of four wickets for 23 runs as Australia stormed back into the game, England slipping to 332 for eight – just 47 ahead.

With only Albert Relf and last man Wilfred Rhodes for company, Foster decided on all-out attack. However, they were hardly the worst "ten-Jack" in history. Relf, a 29-year-old Sussex all-rounder, would score 26 first-class hundreds while Rhodes would hit 58 and open the batting in 27 of his 58 Tests. But with Relf on debut and Rhodes, 26, having only once reached double figures in his eight Test appearances, Foster left nothing to chance. As Relf defended for all he was worth, Foster "hit the Australian bowlers as I am certain they have never before been hit in all the long history of England and Australia matches", said Warner. "It mattered not who bowled; it was all the same to the brilliant batsman." Foster hammered Howell for 13 in an over and lashed 15 off a Laver over. The *Daily Telegraph* reported: "Having played a very safe game on the Saturday, Foster adopted quite different tactics today, batting with great dash and freedom."

Although primarily an artist who relied on timing, Foster could attack with the best of them. In his university days he hit W. G. Grace for four straight sixes, showing England's leviathan paltry regard. At the end of the over Grace walked up and said, "Not very respectful to an old man, was it, 'Tip?'" before adding, "but it was worth seeing". Another time, Foster smashed 262 not out in a club game in 70 minutes while 18 runs came at the other end.

Relf survived for almost 90 minutes then fell in the final over before tea, caught in the slips by Armstrong off Saunders. He'd contributed 31 to a ninth-wicket stand of 115 with Foster, which helped England lift their lead to 162. By now, Foster had passed the highest Test score by an England batsman – K. S. Ranjitsinhji's 175 against Australia at Sydney in 1897. He'd also passed the second-highest individual Test score – Syd Gregory's 201 in the 1894 Sydney Ashes match, when the Australian was ninth out and missed the chance to beat Murdoch. Gregory, a tiny right-hander from New South Wales, was cheered when he beat Charles Bannerman's 165 for the highest Test score made in Australia, showing the rising importance of these and other landmarks now that Test cricket was officially recognised. Bannerman stood in that 1894 game as an umpire, England winning by ten runs after following on – one of only three instances of a side winning a Test in such fashion, the others being

England's defeat of Australia at Headingley in 1981 and India's of Australia at Kolkata in 2001. By quirk of fate, Foster passed Gregory's 201 by cutting Gregory himself for two runs. "Then," wrote Warner, "a few minutes later, amid cheering which W. L. (Billy) Murdoch might have heard in faraway England, he beat that great batsman's 211 at Kennington Oval in 1884."

Warner said that Murdoch's score had stood "on what seemed an inaccessible pinnacle", but Foster not only reached that pinnacle but powered beyond it in company with Rhodes. They added 130, Rhodes contributing 40 to what remained an Ashes record tenth-wicket stand until 2013, when Phillip Hughes and Ashton Agar shared 163 against England at Trent Bridge. Foster was last out, skying left-armer Saunders to Noble at cover. His 287 came in one minute short of seven hours and contained 37 fours. Warner said that Foster's batting on the Monday "was, I think, the best I have ever seen", adding: "His off-driving and cutting have never been equalled – of that I feel sure. On the on-side, too, he was wonderfully good, frequently forcing the ball away in a masterly manner. His style was, as it always is, beautifully easy, and he made good use of his exceptional quickness of foot, frequently moving a yard out of his ground to play the ball... He received a magnificent reception, and the cheering could not have been more genuine had it been at Lord's or The Oval."

Foster's innings took England to 577, a lead of 292. Back home, people did not have to wait long for news of it. During this match, the Pacific cable company transmitted from the SCG to the Central News Agency in London in the record time of three and a half minutes – an "astonishing" achievement, said *Wisden*. One headline announced:

In full flight: R. E. (Record Extinguisher) Foster.

"Foster 287, Australia 285", while another called him "R. E. (Record Extinguisher) Foster". The *London Daily News* declared: "No words of praise are too laudatory for the magnificent feat of R. E. Foster. The MCC have received a full vindication of their judgment in selecting him. When Rhodes came in he pursued the sportsmanlike course of playing for his side. He could easily have carried out his bat, but instead he slashed away at the bowling and did his best to pile on the runs." The *Sydney Referee* said "the first and the last phases in the record innings were as strikingly contrasting in ease, in power, and in brilliancy as anything the mind can conceive. His lifting drives were so extraordinary that they would have put MacLaren's into the shade." Once again, Foster's tour diary illuminated nothing of the pride he must have felt at beating Murdoch. His entry for December 14, 1903, read:

"I got my 100 an over before Braund did. We were both playing well when he was bowled. After lunch Lilley came in but played the fool and was caught. This left us at 332 for 8, which was chucking our position away. Relf came in and played beautifully till he was caught. Meanwhile I had got to 203. After tea Rhodes and I went on and in an hour and ten minutes put on 130 for the last wicket, before I was caught at cover."

Foster's 287 remains the highest score by a Test debutant, the highest for England in Australia and it was the highest Test score at the SCG until 2012, when Michael Clarke struck 329 not out for Australia against India. It was the highest Test score by a visiting batsman in Australia until 2015, when New Zealand's Ross Taylor hit 290 in Perth.

After Foster's record innings, Warner felt that England's lead of almost 300 was "a task before which even such giants as Trumper, Hill, Noble and Duff might well quail". However, he was mindful of the "indomitable pluck and resolution of the Australians", who have "inherited to the full that spirit of never giving in which we are so proud of saying is inherent in the British race". Australia indeed showed indomitable pluck as they moved to 254 for three on the fourth evening, just 38 behind. Hill and Trumper, in fact, seemed to be steering them into a position from which England could conceivably have lost. But at this key stage, Hill was controversially run out after Trumper played a leg-break from Braund past mid-off and the batsmen tried to take a fifth run on an overthrow. Hill was furious at umpire

Bob Crockett's decision and there were groans and hisses in the crowd. Warner walked from his fielding position towards the pavilion with the aim of getting the protests to stop. "But instead of them listening to me, the booing became louder than ever." Noble was next man in, and the Australia captain sat with Warner beside the boundary, hoping that the outcry would end. "During these moments," wrote Warner, "Noble and I were talking the matter over and I told him that we should be compelled to leave the field if the demonstration against Crockett did not cease. After a while the noise abated somewhat, and Noble advised me to go on with the game. The moment we started play, the noise became, if possible, greater than ever, and shouts of 'How much did you pay Crockett, Warner?' – 'Have you got your coffin ready, Crockett?' – 'Which gate are you leaving by, Crockett?' rent the air. It was a most difficult situation, but I think that, on the whole, I acted wisely in not withdrawing the team from the field." Warner said there was "absolutely no excuse" for the demonstrations and that "even such hardened Test match players as Hirst and Rhodes were quite upset", with Crockett needing police protection on leaving the ground.

A cartoon of the run-out incident appeared in an English newspaper portraying "Enthusiastic barracking at Sydney Cricket Ground". It showed a batsman in a suit of armour, fielders hidden beneath manholes, the umpire in a cage, rocks and bottles flying on to the field and the scoreboard keeping tally of the killed and injured. In his tour diary, Foster wrote: "He [Hill] was undoubtedly out as I was standing at short leg and could see. The members started booing and hissing which, of course, was taken up by the rest of the ground and a most disgraceful scene ensued. Though many members tried to excuse it, nothing could make up for the scene." Australia went on to make 485, Trumper scoring an unbeaten 185 and Rhodes returning five for 94. So tirelessly did Rhodes plug away that Trumper at one point complained, "Wilf, won't you give me a bit of peace?" to which the famously taciturn left-arm spinner replied, "No." By common consent, Trumper's innings was better than Foster's, arguably the finest of his career. "It was glory, it was wonder," purred A. A. Thomson. "Old men who saw it recall it with tears, and Australians are not easily moved to tears."

Trumper, 26, was the greatest Australian batsman of the day, renowned for his grace and fluidity of movement. Warner rated him "the finest batsman in the world", saying: "Trumper stands alone; he is like no one, and no one is like him. In repose he is not exactly a stylist, for as he faces the bowler there is a rather ungainly bending of his right knee; but the moment he gets into position to make his stroke he becomes the most brilliant, the most fascinating, and the most attractive bat I have seen." Foster called him "undoubtedly the greatest batsman living and above criticism". No higher praise was given to Foster than when he was called "The English Trumper".

Chasing 194 to win, England were 81 for two when Foster was lured out of his ground by Armstrong and stumped for 19. Braund fell one run later, and England would have been 83 for five – and the match firmly back in the balance – had Hirst not been dropped on nought by Laver at short leg off Howell. Instead, Hirst and opener Hayward carried the tourists to the brink of victory, putting on 99 before Hayward was stumped nine short of a hundred. Hirst finished on 60, England winning a dramatic game by five wickets.

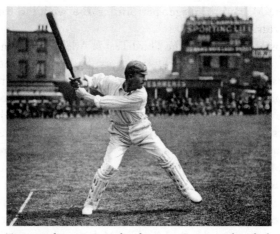

Victor Trumper, the great Australian batsman. Foster was described as "The English Trumper".

On a weather-affected opening day of the Second Test in Melbourne, Foster moved to 49 not out as England reached 221 for two at stumps. However, he complained of a severe chill the next morning, which developed into tonsillitis, and he had to leave the ground before he could resume his innings. "Foster had played so well that it was quite likely that he would have got another three-figure score," said Warner, who described his inability to continue as "a cruel disappointment". England went on to win a low-scoring game by 185 runs to go 2–0 up with three Tests to play, Rhodes returning match figures of 15 for 124 despite having eight catches dropped off him. Foster remained in bed for several days and was nursed through his illness by his wife, Diana. The tour doubled as their honeymoon with Foster's father, Henry, a priest and housemaster at "Tip's" alma mater, Malvern College, performing the wedding earlier that year.

Foster returned for the Third Test in Adelaide, scoring 21 and 16 as England lost by 216 runs. Warner felt that his illness had "left him rather weak" and he was further hampered by a bruised thumb. Foster then returned to the scene of his first Test triumph when England regained the Ashes in the Fourth Test in Sydney. He scored 19 and 27 as the tourists prevailed by 157 runs. There was further crowd trouble when umpire Crockett this time came under fire for not resuming the match earlier after a rain delay. The crowd threw bottles on to the cycle track behind the boundary and littered the area with broken glass. Australia pulled it back to 2–3 by winning the final Test in Melbourne by 218 runs, where Foster hit 18 and 30. He finished as England's leading scorer in the series with 486 and had the highest average of 60.75. Appraising his output, Warner said that Foster was "a little disappointing after his wonderful innings in the first Test match, but ill-health probably had something to do with this".

Having led England to their first Ashes series victory for eight years, Warner could reflect on a job well done after pre-tour criticism concerning his appointment. He'd created an excellent team spirit with amateurs and professionals staying together in the same hotels in a break from precedent and had won the respect of his players. Bosanquet called him "a wise and most successful captain" with "tact and kindly influence", while MacLaren, having declined to tour under him, now praised his "pluck and determined nature". *Punch* captured the mood of a nation that wrongly wrote off Warner and co:

Foster the footballer pictured with Corinthians F. C. in 1901. He is first left on the middle row and C. B. Fry, the Sussex and England batsman, fourth left on the back row.

There once was a skipper named Plum
Whose team made the prophets all glum
"It's bad through and through"
They declared "it won't do"
But today all those prophets are dumb

Foster next played for England over three years later. He was chosen as captain for a three-match series against South Africa in 1907, which England won 1–0. Although he made a half-century in the final game at The Oval, Foster never again approached the heights of Sydney 1903. After that Oval Test he played only two more first-class games as Stock Exchange work took increasing priority.

Foster's footballing career also declined. In the early 1900s he played for Corinthians, a well-known London amateur club. C. B. Fry, the Sussex and England batsman and one of his footballing team-mates, remembered him as "quick without being fast", saying: "He had fine dexterity of foot, and controlled the ball, caressed and persuaded it with an almost manual cunning. His feet had, as it were, the Oxford accent."

Like Trumper, who died in 1915, aged 37, from the kidney disorder Bright's Disease, Foster died tragically young. He contracted consumption (tuberculosis) following on from diabetes in the days before insulin could stabilise the condition. A trip to South Africa a year before his death brought no improvement, so he returned to London, with poor health having dogged him since his severe chill on the 1903-04 Ashes tour.

Foster died on May 13, 1914, shortly after his 36th birthday, the sad news reaching Lord's while MCC were playing Yorkshire. At MCC's annual meeting the following year, Lord Hawke paid him this tribute: "The early death of 'Tip' Foster was a great blow to the whole cricket world. His 287 at Sydney will never be forgotten as long as cricket is played." Hawke added that Foster would "always be remembered for his gentleness of character" – a sentiment echoed by C. B. Fry, who said that he was "a fine example of what should be connoted by the old-fashioned term, an English gentleman".

Foster was cremated at Golders Green and his ashes taken home to Malvern. His funeral was attended by representatives of many sports and sporting bodies. Among the 150 floral tributes was a laurel wreath from his old captain, Plum Warner. Referencing his world record Test score, it bore the simple and touching salute:

"To 'Tip', from 'Plum'.
Sydney, December 14, 1903"

Australia v England

Played at Sydney Cricket Ground on 11, 12, 14, 15, 16, 17 December, 1903.
Toss: Australia. Result: England won by five wickets.

AUSTRALIA

R. A. Duff c Lilley b Arnold	3 –	(3) c Relf b Rhodes	84
V. T. Trumper c Foster b Arnold	1 –	(5) not out	185
C. Hill c Lilley b Hirst	5 –	(4) run out (Relf/Lilley)	51
*M. A. Noble c Foster b Arnold	133 –	(6) st Lilley b Bosanquet	22
W. W. Armstrong b Bosanquet	48 –	(7) c Bosanquet b Rhodes	27
A. J. Y. Hopkins b Hirst	39 –	(8) c Arnold b Rhodes	20
W. P. Howell c Relf b Arnold	5 –	(10) c Lilley b Arnold	4
S. E. Gregory b Bosanquet	23 –	(1) c Lilley b Rhodes	43
F. J. Laver lbw b Rhodes	4 –	c Relf b Rhodes	6
†J. J. Kelly c Braund b Rhodes	10 –	(2) b Arnold	13
J. V. Saunders not out	11 –	run out (Hirst/Rhodes/Lilley)	2
Nb 3	3	B 10, lb 15, w 2, nb 1	28

1/2 (2) 2/9 (1) 3/12 (3)   (118.2 overs) 285
4/118 (5) 5/200 (6) 6/207 (7)
7/259 (8) 8/263 (9) 9/271 (4) 10/285 (10)

1/36 (2) 2/108 (1)   (145.2 overs) 485
3/191 (3) 4/254 (4)
5/334 (6) 6/393 (7) 7/441 (8)
8/468 (9) 9/473 (10) 10/485 (11)

Hirst 24–8–47–2; Arnold 32–7–76–4; Braund 26–9–39–0;
Rhodes 17.2–3–41–2; Relf 6–1–27–0. *Second innings—* Hirst 29–1–79–0; Arnold 28–2–93–2;
Rhodes 40.2–10–94–5; Bosanquet 23–1–100–1; Braund 12–2–56–0; Relf 13–5–35–0.

ENGLAND

T. W. Hayward b Howell	15 –	st Kelly b Saunders	91
*P. F. Warner c Kelly b Laver	0 –	b Howell	8
J. T. Tyldesley b Noble	53 –	c Noble b Saunders	9
E. G. Arnold c Laver b Armstrong	27		
R. E. Foster c Noble b Saunders	287 –	(4) st Kelly b Armstrong	19
L. C. Braund b Howell	102 –	(5) c Noble b Howell	0
G. H. Hirst b Howell	0 –	(6) not out	60
B. J. T. Bosanquet c Howell b Noble	2 –	(7) not out	1
†A. F. A. Lilley c Hill b Noble	4		
A. E. Relf c Armstrong b Saunders	31		
W. Rhodes not out	40		
B 6, lb 7, w 1, nb 2	16	B 3, lb 1, w 2	6

1/0 (2) 2/49 (1) 3/73 (3)   (181.2 overs) 577
4/117 (4) 5/309 (6) 6/311 (7)
7/318 (8) 8/332 (9) 9/447 (10) 10/577 (5)

1/21 (2)   (5 wkts, 95.5 overs) 194
2/39 (3) 3/81 (4)
4/82 (5) 5/181 (1)

Saunders 36.2–8–125–2; Laver 37–12–119–1; Howell 31–7–111–3; Noble 34–8–99–3;
Armstrong 23–3–47–1; Hopkins 11–1–40–0; Trumper 7–2–12–0; Gregory 2–0–8–0.
Second innings— Noble 12–2–37–0; Howell 31–18–35–2; Saunders 18.5–3–51–2;
Laver 16–4–37–0; Armstrong 18–6–28–1.

Umpires: R. M. Crockett and A. C. Jones.

4

Andy Sandham (325)
England versus West Indies
Jamaica 1930

On December 14, 1929, the anniversary date of "Tip" Foster's record, England embarked on their maiden Test tour to the West Indies. It was notable not only for the fact that it was their first such visit to the Caribbean, but also that it was one of two England Test tours that happened simultaneously. While Freddie Calthorpe's men were in the West Indies, Harold Gilligan's side were in New Zealand. At one point, England played two Tests on opposite sides of the world at the same time, a unique occurrence. The double booking was motivated not by money; there was no television cash in those days or different formats to cram into a saturated schedule. Rather, it reflected a desire to expand Test cricket which, before 1928, had been played only by Australia, England and South Africa. In 1926, West Indies and New Zealand had been elected to the Imperial Cricket Conference (forerunner of the International Cricket Council), which made them eligible to play Tests. MCC wanted to send sides to both countries as soon as possible but were constrained by existing commitments in Australia and South Africa, hence the idea for two tours at once. However, with England having recently undertaken a seven-month trip to Australia, first-choice amateurs and professionals were disinclined to spend more time away. The appointment of the uncapped 33-year-old Sussex batsman Gilligan to lead the squad to New Zealand reflected this, and was more a reward for his service to the game than especially meritorious in a cricketing sense. In addition to the famous 42-year-old Kent all-rounder Frank Woolley, Gilligan's squad included only four others with international experience, each of whom had just one cap. The primary purpose of the tour was to promote Test cricket in New Zealand, which received a boost despite the fact that England won the four-match series 1–0.

Freddie Calthorpe, for his part, was a 37-year-old all-rounder from Warwickshire and also an uncapped captain. The Honourable Frederick Somerset Gough Calthorpe, to give him his Sunday name, was son of Lord Calthorpe and heir to the title. An amateur whose diplomatic skills were considered as important in this case as his cricketing ones, Calthorpe had useful knowledge of the West Indian islands having led an MCC visit four years earlier. He also had a better squad than Gilligan, with West Indies having shown their potential in unofficial games against England in the 1920s, despite losing 3–0 on their maiden Test tour to England in 1928.

To say that Calthorpe's squad was on the geriatric side of experienced, however, is an understatement. Wilfred Rhodes, the non-striker when "Tip" Foster beat Billy Murdoch's record, was 52 and remains the oldest Test cricketer. George Gunn, the Nottinghamshire opening batsman, was 50 and had last played for England in 1912. In addition, Nigel Haig, a swing-bowling all-rounder from Middlesex, was 42; Ewart Astill, a medium-pacer/middle-order batsman from Leicestershire, 41; Patsy Hendren, a Middlesex batsman and still an England regular, 40; Rony Stanyforth, a Yorkshire batsman/wicketkeeper, 37, and Jack O'Connor, an Essex batsman/spinner, 32. Only the Nottinghamshire pace bowler Bill Voce (20), Kent wicketkeeper Les Ames (24), Derbyshire all-rounder Leslie Townsend (26), Warwickshire batsman Bob Wyatt (28) and Middlesex all-rounder Greville Stevens (29) were the right side of 30. Another veteran was the diminutive Surrey opener Andy Sandham (39), who'd played the last of his ten Tests in 1925.

Born in Streatham, south London, in 1890, Sandham was Jack Hobbs's opening partner at Surrey. Like Hobbs he was entirely self-taught; in his case, via Saturday-afternoon cricket on Streatham Common. The son of a gardener, Sandham joined Mitcham CC before gaining trials at Surrey and winning a place on The Oval groundstaff. He made his first-class debut just before his 21st birthday in 1911, scoring 53 in an innings win against Cambridge University. As a youngster, Sandham modelled himself on Tom Hayward, whom he succeeded as Hobbs's partner. The powerful Hayward, who opened in "Tip" Foster's match, scored 43,551 first-class runs and 104 hundreds, *Wisden* describing him as "one of the greatest batsmen of all time". Five foot six and fast on his feet, Sandham was more of a touch player, the writer and broadcaster John Arlott recalling "a dapper, poised, unspectacular but outstandingly equipped batsman, unflinching against pace, quick of wit and movement in dealing with spin". Errol Holmes, one of his captains at Surrey, said that Sandham's shots "were executed with confidence and a sort of finality", adding: "I doubt if there has ever been a greater player of the deflection strokes."

Sandham's career was interrupted by the Great War, which started when he was 24 and yet to establish himself. He served in the Sportsman's Battalions, the Royal Fusiliers, along with Patsy Hendren, his team-mate on the 1929-30 West Indies tour. Private Sandham had cause to be grateful for a bout of appendicitis that spared him the horror of the Somme. It required an operation and his repatriation before the Fusiliers went into action at Delville Wood, where thousands died.

When county cricket returned in 1919, after a gap of over four and a half years, Sandham made up for lost time. He continued playing first-class cricket until shortly after his 47th birthday, joining a select band – headed by Hobbs – to score 100 first-class hundreds. Sandham hit 107 and then played well into retirement, turning out for London Counties in representative games in the Second World War. London Counties were mainly made up of old southern professionals and provided entertainment for a sports-starved public while raising funds for war charities. The club president was Hobbs, who'd played his final first-class match in 1934 and retired with a world-record 61,237 runs and 197 hundreds at an average of 50.65.*

Five years earlier, Hobbs's absence from the 1929-30 West Indies tour was a PR blow for the hosts, with representatives from the Jamaican board having visited London in the summer of 1929 in an effort to persuade him

---

* The Association of Cricket Statisticians subsequently declared matches that Hobbs played on a private tour to Ceylon (Sri Lanka) to be first-class, giving him 61,760 runs at 50.70 with 199 hundreds. However, Wisden does not recognise these games as first-class, hence the figures followed for Hobbs in this book and the discrepancy with some statistical sources.

to travel. But Hobbs turned 47 in December 1929 and the selectors wanted him to rest before the 1930 Ashes, which would prove his international swansong. The West Indies tour would prove Sandham's international swansong too, his world-record 325 in the Fourth and final Test in Jamaica not the worst way to bow out.

Prior to the tour, Sandham had only once passed fifty in 15 Test innings dating back to his debut against Warwick Armstrong's Australians in 1921. He'd had a tough time in the 1924-25 Ashes, managing only 28 runs in four innings as an England team led by Harold Gilligan's elder brother, Arthur, was thumped 4–1. And he'd looked on in frustration as Yorkshire's Herbert Sutcliffe had become Hobbs's regular opening partner in Tests – just as Percy Holmes, Sutcliffe's opening partner at Yorkshire, felt similarly stymied. Now, handed one last hurrah by MCC's mission to *spread the word*, Sandham was determined to enjoy every minute. While Hobbs and Sutcliffe took a well-earned break, he got to work as a key member of Calthorpe's ageing crew.

Sandham started the series as he meant to go on, scoring a hundred in the drawn First Test in Barbados – West Indies' first home Test match. After the hosts scored 369, attacking opener Clifford Roach striking their first century (122), Sandham top-scored with 152 as England replied with 467. George Headley, a precocious 20-year-old who came to be known as "The Black Bradman", hit 176 on debut as West Indies followed up with 384, leaving England 287 to win in a little under three hours. They didn't attempt it, Sandham top-scoring again with 51 as they finished on 167 for three. Sandham came down to earth in the Second Test in Trinidad, making nought and five as England won by 167 runs to go

1–0 up. He remained grounded during the third game in Guyana, falling for nine and nought as West Indies levelled with a 289-run win, their first Test victory. Roach scored a double-century, the imperious Headley a hundred in each innings and fast-bowling all-rounder Learie Constantine took nine wickets.

With the series locked at 1–1, it was decided that the final Test would be timeless and played to a finish. This was nothing new; if the series result hinged on it, the final game would often be timeless, with Tests in Australia having long been played to a conclusion. However, a conse-

JAMAICA AND WEST INDIES XI.

"The Black Bradman" – West Indies' batsman George Headley, who scored four hundreds and 703 runs at 87.87 in his maiden Test series against England in 1930.

quence was that batsmen sometimes forsook their natural game to adopt a more conservative approach. With no need to get on with it, and with groundsmen skilled at producing pitches to last, the cricket was sometimes less than compelling. The pitch at Sabina Park, Jamaica, for the all-important decider was certainly produced to last. Sandham remembered a "beautiful clay wicket" on which the bowlers "never had a chance".

Calthorpe won the toss and asked Sandham and Gunn to put on their pads. According to reports, play began in "agreeable weather before a large and excited crowd". That West Indies were viewed as minor opposition was reflected in newspaper coverage of the series in England. The media

The England players before the Jamaica Test. Left to right: Patsy Hendren, George Gunn, Wilfred Rhodes, Les Ames, Bill Voce, Bob Wyatt, Freddie Calthorpe (captain), Nigel Haig, Ewart Astill, Andy Sandham, Jack O'Connor.

carried sparse reports under the heading "*PA* Foreign Special", most of which seemed cobbled from the scorecard. The concurrent New Zealand tour was similarly treated, Harold Gilligan's squad arriving back in Southampton on the opening day of the Jamaica Test.

England made one change from the Third Test in Georgetown, Jack O'Connor replacing fellow all-rounder Leslie Townsend. Also omitted was Fred Price, a 27-year-old Middlesex wicketkeeper who'd been sent for as back-up to Les Ames after a bizarre injury to Rony Stanyforth. While shaving one morning, Stanyforth cut himself so badly that he almost lopped off one of his fingers. Despite their maiden Test win in Georgetown, West Indies made a whopping nine changes, batting heroes Roach and Headley the only survivors. This apparently absurd move was because each venue had a different selection panel (West Indies used 27 players during the series, including a different white captain from the colony that staged each Test). Left-handed opener Karl Nunes did the honours in Jamaica, having led West Indies on their tour to England in 1928. His side at Sabina Park was packed with fellow Jamaicans, four of whom – wicketkeeper Ivan Barrow, all-rounder Oscar Da Costa, left-arm spinner George Gladstone and batsman Clarence Passailaigue – were on debut. There was a five-week gap between the Third and Fourth Tests, reflecting the more sedate nature of tours in those days. The four Tests were spread out over three months, with England also playing nine tour games of mostly four days' duration.

Despite the pristine batting conditions, England did not get away from their hosts on the first day in Jamaica, but nor were they in much trouble. Against a modest attack, with only fast bowler Herman Griffith and leg-spinner Tommy Scott posing much threat, the action followed the usual pattern of timeless Tests, with batsmen concerned with laying foundations. Not that Sandham was ever a dashing batsman, the sort to add flair to the foundation stone. R. C. Robertson-Glasgow called him "primarily the servant of his art and his team, only secondarily the entertainer of the public", while Neville Cardus scoffed: "Frankly, I cannot get enthusiastic about the cricket of a Sandham, a Hearne, a Sutcliffe. I was not brought up amongst cricketers who got their runs by waiting for a very bad ball, then hitting it to the boundary – after lunch."

In Jamaica, where England lunched on a leisurely 69 for nought, Sandham and Gunn were as careful as motorists on an icy road. They played more freely after the break, as if to bring Cardus's words to life, although "the bowling was never completely mastered". In the end, it took a rush of blood from Gunn to bring the first wicket just before tea with the total standing at 173. Tempted to "go out for one", as the "*PA* Foreign Special" put it, by the left-arm spin of Freddie Martin, Gunn was stumped by Barrow to end "a flawless innings of 85". As Gunn trudged off, Sandham quipped that it would have been nice if he'd scored a Test century at his age, to which the quinquagenarian returned, "Perhaps, but I thought that if one of us didn't get out, we wouldn't catch the boat home."

Gunn, whose uncle John and elder brother William also played for Nottinghamshire and England, was often tempted to "go out for one". Not that this was any guarantee that he'd try and score runs; indeed, Gunn seemed to take perverse pleasure in trying to hit only the most difficult deliveries and blocking those he could have clobbered with ease. *Wisden* bemoaned: "Rarely when he left his ground in this way did his skill betray him and yet, though obviously so completely at home that he could have done almost anything with the ball, he would make a stroke which sent it tamely to the bowler, to mid-off or to mid-on. In match after match this practice of merely killing the ball was indulged in to such an extent as to become almost an obsession. It appeared to furnish Gunn with complete satisfaction, but it occasioned considerable annoyance to spectators who knew that, if he wished, he could score both without undue effort and as rapidly as anybody."

Sandham had now been joined by Bob Wyatt and had 96 out of 184 for one at tea. Having scored only 14 runs in the previous two Tests, "Sandy" was back in form and closing in on a third hundred in nine days after innings of 155 and 126 in warm-up games against Jamaica.

As he neared three figures at Sabina Park, some three months short of his 40th birthday, it was not so much the nervous nineties for Sandham as the painful ones. He was suffering from sore feet and wearing a pair of Patsy Hendren's boots as his own were too tight. The replacement boots didn't fit properly and kept slipping as he ran quick singles. Once a boot came off in the middle of the pitch with funny as opposed to fatal results. The pain grew increasingly worse and, when he brought up his hundred, Sandham told umpire Joe Hardstaff, the former Nottinghamshire and England batsman, that he'd have a dart and get out if necessary. "Why not get your 150 first, Andy?" said Hardstaff, who urged him to forget about the pain in his boots and to fill them instead. Sandham reached 150 just before stumps – England closing day one on 289 for one – and then further signalled he'd had enough. Again, Hardstaff pressed: "Get 200 before you go."

On day two, Sandham reached his double-hundred and the back-and-forth dialogue continued, Hardstaff telling him he had a wonderful chance to beat "Tip" Foster's record. Until then, Sandham had not been conscious of it, his thoughts entirely dominated by the comforting one of soaking his feet in a nice warm bath. He was winging it now in more ways than one, for as well as wearing Hendren's boots he was using a bat borrowed from captain Calthorpe as his own had broken early in the innings (Sandham's spares had also broken or been sold to locals as the tour wound down). "It was not a bat I would have chosen myself," he said. "It was a long handle, for a start, and I didn't like the balance of it."

Sandham pictured early in his career.

England lost one wicket on the second morning in reaching 404 for two at lunch, Wyatt caught behind off Da Costa's medium-pace for 58 to end a stand with Sandham of 148. Hendren hammered a brisk 61 either side of the break, adding 97 with Sandham for the third wicket before falling to a well-judged catch at deep mid-off by Passailaigue off Scott. Sandham, sporting a panama to protect himself from the afternoon sun, was then joined by Ames, some 15 years his junior. One of the game's great wicketkeeper/batsmen, who'd score 102 first-class hundreds and claim 1,121 dismissals, Ames arrived in the mood for quick singles. It soon became too much for Sandham, who demurred: "Now look here, Les, it's all right for you, but I've been in for hours and I'm in my 40th year." By tea, they'd lifted the score to 563 for three, Sandham's share of 255 having taken him past the highest Test score since Foster – Wally Hammond's 251 for England against Australia at Sydney the previous winter. Hammond missed the chance to beat the record when seventh out in England's first-innings 636, bowled by 45-year-old left-arm spinner Bert Ironmonger.

As Sandham closed in on history beneath the Blue Mountains, which provided a stunning backdrop to the sparsely appointed venue, there was no sense of occasion at the ground or back in England. There was no reference in the "*PA Foreign Special*" reports, for example, to a single shot that he played in his innings – never mind the prospect of him beating Foster. Indeed, the prevailing view in England was that this wasn't really a Test series at all, but rather a goodwill mission by a scratch England squad to support a fledgling cricketing power. The English cricket writer A. W. Pullin – aka "Old Ebor" – summed it up when he described the Jamaica match as a "so-called Test" and a "wearisome farce", adding: "The only real Tests in the estimate of the British home public remain those in which England, Australia and Africa are concerned." Pullin maintained that the playing of Tests between England and West Indies was "a mistake" and that the side in Jamaica had "no real right to be regarded as representative of England's cricketing strength".

If umpire Hardstaff was cognisant of Foster's record, it seemed that no one else took much notice when Sandham

passed it on the second evening to an absolute absence of
fuss and fanfare. If anything, it was Ames's work that was
praised, the Kent man registering what *Wisden* termed "a
capital hundred". Ames's 149 was the highest of his eight
Test centuries – a riotous romp in 174 balls and two hours,
ten minutes. Bowled by a quick delivery from Griffith, Ames
contributed the lion's share of a stand of 249 with Sandham
that left England 667 for four.

Having taken the record almost by stealth, Sandham
sized up the first triple-hundred of his career after two
near misses playing for Surrey. In 1921, he was on 292
against Northamptonshire at The Oval when his captain,
Percy Fender, declared overnight, a decision that left him
thoroughly brassed off. In 1928, Sandham was on 282 against
Lancashire at Old Trafford when he had to retire ill with
breathing difficulty. This time, though, it was third time
lucky as "Sandy" achieved the first Test triple, ending day
two on 309 out of 700 for four (Jack O'Connor 22).

With no imperative for Calthorpe to declare, Sandham
dragged his sore feet back to the crease on day three preceded
by the no less weary bowlers. It was an inexperienced attack
with one of its number, spinner Gladstone, making his second
and last first-class appearance. Without Constantine's speed,
the bowling was blunt, and although Scott spun his way to
five wickets, the 37-year-old conceded 266 runs in the
process, then the most in a Test innings. Griffith, 36, was the
likeliest threat, and the tireless paceman – as strong as an ox –
finally ended Sandham's marathon. Pushing at a ball outside
his off stump, he played on, saying: "I got a bit careless."

Sandham's dismissal left England 720 for five. He'd batted
for ten hours and faced 640 balls, striking 28 fours, one seven

The Sabina Park scoreboard shows Sandham's new record.

and one five (both the result of overthrows), eight threes, 23 twos and 131 singles. Rather than praise his efforts, most writers panned them. A. W. Pullin sneered: "Those acquainted with the cricket usually played by Sandham would not expect him to develop a galloping pace in the scoring sense, even when well set. In the match in Jamaica the reports state that the Surrey batsman was at the wicket about ten hours, and scored 325 out of 720 runs made in that time. Possibly we should make some allowance for the effect of the West Indies climate upon Europeans; it is not likely to develop sprinting qualities between the wickets, for example. Still an average of 30 runs an hour for ten hours is a very sedate trot indeed, and I cannot imagine any West Indies cricket lover, whether white or of colour, waxing enthusiastic over the performance."

Sandham certainly exhibited few "sprinting qualities" in this innings and practically limped from the crease due to his feet. The following winter he experienced more problems with them on England's tour to South Africa, which prevented him from adding to his Test appearances. Chosen as part of another scratch squad, Sandham was injured in a car accident early in the trip. "I was being driven back to the hotel in Durban late one night after a dance," he said. "We drove over a bridge, and I turned round to look at the bridge to see what it looked like when it was lit up, and whilst I turned round something happened. When I came to, I found myself in a tiny little room with a big police sergeant in one corner and a woman in another corner holding her arm, and sundry other people on the right. I went off again, and found myself in hospital. I'd been cut over the eyes and had pain in the ribs and an arm. When I got to Cape Town Percy Chapman said I must get my ankle X-rayed. This showed a broken bone in my heel. As for my host, who was driving, I think the poor chap got the sack." As a kind of gruesome souvenir, Sandham came home with part of his heel bone pickled in a bottle.

Sandham's was the first of five wickets that England lost on the third morning at Sabina Park, the visitors lunching on 834 for nine. The innings finally ended at 849 when Bill Voce became Scott's fifth victim, caught in the deep by Da Costa. England's score was the highest in Test cricket, beating their 636 against Australia at Sydney the previous winter. But it cut no ice with A. W. Pullin, who said that "the policy of rubbing it in against tired bowlers has not much to commend it".

Nunes top-scored with 66 as West Indies made 286 in reply, giving England a lead of 563. There followed one of the most infamous decisions in cricketing history. With the match in the closing stages of day four, and with West Indies beaten in everything but fact, Calthorpe chose not to enforce the follow-on, reasoning that "there were five and a half days left for play [before England had to catch the boat home] and the prospect was that the wicket was bound to break up". Perhaps the age of his team had something to do with it; the average age was 37, and England had just spent a long, tiring day in the field. But it was still an incredibly cautious move, a bit like taking an umbrella into the Sahara on the off-chance of a shower. Sandham recalled asking the lean and lanky Calthorpe – "a charming chap", in the words of Bob Wyatt – whether he wanted him to open again. "He said, 'No, that's all right, Andy. How about No. 7?' I said that was fine, but I still had to go in." Sandham scored 50 out of 272 for nine declared, lifting his match tally to 375 – a record until Australia's Greg Chappell scored 247 and 133 (aggregate 380) against New Zealand at Wellington in 1974. Calthorpe's tactic left West Indies 836 to win – "an appalling task", commented *Wisden*.

The hosts began their ordeal on the sixth morning, Nunes and Headley making a terrific fist of things in guiding them to 234 for one at stumps. Headley, whose slight build belied a dominant method, reached his fourth hundred of the series and advanced to 223 on day seven before being stumped off Wyatt's medium-pace. Nunes went on to 92 as West Indies finished that day on 408 for five, not yet halfway to their hideous target. Only rain could possibly have saved them and, on cue, it arrived with a vengeance, with no play possible on days eight or nine before England indeed had to catch the boat home. The pitch was now in a laughable state. "When they took the covers off you never saw such a sight," said Sandham. "Yellow weeds springing up all over. No one would have believed it was a Test wicket." And so the game and the series was drawn, the Test not so "timeless" that shipping schedules could be overlooked (the same thing happened nine years later in the last timeless Test when England – chasing 696 to beat South Africa in Durban – were 654 for five on day ten when they, too, had to catch their ship). Sandham ended the tour with 1,281 runs from 12 first-class games at 64.05 with only Hendren (1,765 at 135.76) scoring more. By the start of the 1930 summer, though, he was out of the international picture again. For the visit of Australia, his world-record 325 counted for nothing as Hobbs and Sutcliffe resumed their stand.

Like the dutiful plod to the dazzling detective, the Chief Inspector Japp to Hercule Poirot, Sandham existed in Hobbs's shadow. He accepted rather than resented it, stoically serving as junior partner. Their association lasted for 15 years and yielded 66 century stands, with a highest of 428 against Oxford University at The Oval in 1926. Echoing his desire to get out when his feet were hurting at Sabina Park, this stand only ended when Sandham took pity on the undergraduates and deliberately threw his wicket away. Hobbs was also known for doing this, giving others a chance after reaching three figures. It reflected his kindly nature and innate sense of fairness, which made him popular with one and all. A classical batsman of medium height, Hobbs was known simply as "The Master". Born into poverty in 1882, the eldest of 12 children, he went on to become the first professional cricketer to be knighted. Shorter and stockier than his famous partner, Sandham was the ideal foil. R. C. Robertson-Glasgow called him "a first fiddle who, for most of his time, played second in the orchestra... Or, if you like, he was the magician Hobbs' assistant; sharing in the show and most necessary to it; far removed from the 'anonymous bloke' whose hand is sometimes seen in the wings throwing in a hoop or some property of illusion; regarded with esteem and affection not only by the master but by the discerning audience. Yet, because of the unalterable injustice of circumstance, he was generally standing just on the shadow side of the spotlight while the applause at last died away and the spectators chattered of the greatness they had seen."

Sandham marvelled at Hobbs's greatness, his ability to thrive in all conditions, and said of batting with him: "It is a curious experience. The attention of the crowd is centred entirely on Hobbs. I feel that from the moment I leave the pavilion. The runs I score are hardly noticed." Once, Sandham scored a hundred and Hobbs was out first ball. The news placards read: "Hobbs out for o at The Oval". As Sandham said: "I suppose you've got to be a pretty good player to merit a contents bill when you've got a duck." But he didn't begrudge Hobbs his success and admired his modesty. "He's a fine chap. If he'd been at all swollen-headed he would have been unbearable because at the time, you know, the newspapers were all Jack Hobbs this, that and the other. But he was a grand fellow... He was nice to everybody." Sandham accepted that Hobbs took the headlines, "but it used to annoy my wife, who didn't know anything about cricket at all. She'd say, 'Well, there are ten other people playing besides Jack Hobbs.'"

The openers had telepathic awareness. "I think twice there was a run-out," said Sandham. "We never called; we looked and went. I knew Jack wanted a run as soon as he shaped for his push on the off side and I was a yard or so down the wicket as soon as the ball was bowled." Sandham was always vigilant off the final ball of an over especially, with Hobbs renowned for stealing the strike. "Very often, Hobbs would say to me, 'Let me have most of the bowling if you can; I just feel like batting today,' which I thought was rather funny because he always felt like it." Consequently, when Sandham played for England, he liked to pinch the strike himself. Bob Wyatt said: "I jokingly complained to him, to which he retorted that he'd had to put up with a lot of that from Jack Hobbs and he didn't see why he shouldn't get his own back now." The comment was typical of Sandham, who was usually armed with a quip or two. Arthur Carr, the former Nottinghamshire and England captain, said that Sandham had "a most dry and amusing sense of humour", while Henry Grierson, a Surrey-born left-arm bowler, remembered Sandham's "grand" wit, adding: "I never heard him say an

Jack Hobbs, left, and Andy Sandham walking out to bat for Surrey against Kent at Blackheath in 1925. They put on 199 – one of 66 century stands that they shared for the first wicket.

unkind thing about anyone during our 58 years of friendship."
Hobbs himself said: "We had some great times together. He
was full of dry humour and we must have run more short
singles than I did with Wilfred [Rhodes] and Herbert
[Sutcliffe] put together. He had a lovely off-drive and his late
cut was worth walking miles to see, and he was always a very
good friend."

Off the field, Sandham was more outgoing than Hobbs,
but more serious on it compared to his partner. The writer
Ronald Mason said: "Sandham was blessed with a curiously
Mongolian cast of countenance; under the shady peak of his
cap his eyes hooded themselves watchfully, never blinking,
always alert, a little mysterious, inscrutable. Unlike his
partner, who had at rare moments a slow and rather appealing
grin, Sandham was not seen to smile; it disturbed his
methodical concentration. Instead, he sported a thoughtful
frown, preoccupied and absorbed, advertising a purposeful
determination that he put resolutely into practice."

Sandham played 643 first-class matches, scoring 41,284 runs
at an average of 44.82. After resting the sore feet of a career
that spanned 26 years, he served Surrey as coach and then as
scorer, his association with them lasting for over 60 years.
Sandham was coach when Surrey won a record seven
successive County Championships in the 1950s, modestly
stating that "the first XI didn't want much looking after".
According to R. C. Robertson-Glasgow, he "gave all that he
could to cricket, and took less from it than he deserved".

Sandham lived his last years not far from Lord's, his 325
bat propped up in a corner of a room. He died on April 20,
1982, less than three months short of his 92nd birthday. That
bat meant much to him, even though he was something of a

forgotten holder of the highest Test score, a man whose achievement was looked down on/scarcely acknowledged. Sandham performed it while effectively playing for an England reserve team against weak opposition, using somebody else's boots and somebody else's bat, on a docile pitch that developed yellow weeds. There was an element of village green about it; one wouldn't have been entirely surprised if some of the fielders had not worn whites.

Public apathy was reflected in the muted reception that Sandham and his colleagues received. They returned home at the end of April 1930 to empty railway stations and widespread disinterest, one report stating that "they crept into London almost furtively at a time when platform sweepers and a few belated Cup final revellers were almost the only other people visible". It was all in stark contrast to the welcome afforded to the Australian team when they'd arrived in England four days earlier, with over 5,000 greeting them ahead of the Ashes. Among their number was a boy wonder who would not only break Sandham's record within weeks, but pretty much rewrite the entire record book before he was through.

West Indies v England

Played at Sabina Park, Kingston, Jamaica, on 3, 4, 5, 7, 8, 9, 10, 11, 12 April, 1930.
Toss: England. Result: Match drawn.

ENGLAND

G. Gunn st Barrow b Martin	85	– run out (Martin)	47
A. Sandham b Griffith	325	– (7) lbw b Griffith	50
R. E. S. Wyatt c Barrow b Da Costa	58	– (2) c Passailaigue b Da Costa	10
E. H. Hendren c Passailaigue b Scott	61	– b Roach.	55
†L. E. G. Ames b Griffith.	149	– c Nunes b Scott	27
J. O'Connor c Da Costa b Scott	51	– (3) c Headley b Scott	3
*F. S. G. Calthorpe c Griffith b Scott	5	– (8) st Barrow b Scott	8
N. E. Haig c Da Costa b Gladstone	28	– (6) c Passailaigue b Scott	34
W. E. Astill b Scott	39	– b Griffith.	10
W. Rhodes not out.	8	– not out	11
W. Voce c Da Costa b Scott.	20	– not out	6
B 6, lb 12, w 1, nb 1	20	B 5, lb 6.	11

1/173 (1) 2/321 (3) 3/418 (4)   (258.2 overs) 849   1/22 (2)   (9 wkts dec, 79.1 overs) 272
4/667 (5) 5/720 (2) 6/748 (7)   2/35 (3) 3/116 (4)
7/755 (6) 8/813 (8) 9/821 (9) 10/849 (11)   4/121 (1) 5/176 (5) 6/180 (6)
                                                       7/198 (8) 8/233 (9) 9/256 (7)

Griffith 58–6–155–2; Da Costa 21–0–81–1; Gladstone 42–5–139–1; Scott 80.2–13–266–5;
Martin 45–6–128–1; Headley 5–0–23–0; Roach 5–0–22–0; Passailaigue 2–0–15–0.
Second innings – Griffith 21.1–5–52–2; Da Costa 6–2–14–1; Gladstone 8–0–50–0;
Scott 25–0–108–4; Martin 9–1–12–0; Roach 10–1–25–1.

WEST INDIES

*R. K. Nunes c Ames b Voce.	66	– b Astill	92
C. A. Roach lbw b Haig	15	– c Gunn b Rhodes	22
G. A. Headley c Haig b Voce.	10	– st Ames b Wyatt.	223
F. R. Martin lbw b Haig.	33	– (5) c Sandham b Wyatt	24
F. I. de Caires run out (Voce/Ames)	21	– (4) b Haig	16
C. C. Passailaigue b Haig.	44	– not out	2
†I. M. Barrow b Astill.	0		
O. C. Da Costa c Haig b Astill.	39		
O. C. Scott c and b Astill	8		
H. C. Griffith c Hendren b Rhodes	7		
G. Gladstone not out	12		
B 19, lb 5, w 2, nb 5	31	B 17, lb 11, nb 1	29

1/53 (2) 2/80 (3) 3/141 (1)   (111.5 overs) 286   1/44 (2)   (5 wkts, 164.3 overs) 408
4/156 (4) 5/181 (5) 6/181 (7)   2/271 (1) 3/320 (4)
7/254 (6) 8/265 (9) 9/270 (8) 10/286 (10)   4/397 (3) 5/408 (5)

Voce 22–3–81–2; Haig 30–10–73–3; Rhodes 20.5–12–17–1; Astill 33–12–73–3;
Wyatt 4–0–11–0; O'Connor 2–2–0–0. *Second innings* – Voce 29–3–94–0; Haig 26–15–49–1;
Rhodes 24–13–22–1; Astill 46–13–108–1; Wyatt 24.3–7–58–2; O'Connor 11–3–32–0;
Calthorpe 4–1–16–0.

Umpires: J. Hardstaff snr and E. Knibbs.

Don Bradman (334)
Australia versus England
Headingley 1930

Percy Fender wasn't convinced. After the 1928-29 Ashes, he had doubts about an Australian batsman who'd made his debut in the opening Test. "Bradman was one of the most curious mixtures of good and bad batting I have ever seen," asserted the Surrey captain. "One minute one would think him a good player, and the next he would look like a schoolboy… He makes a mistake, then makes it again and again; he does not correct it, or look as if he were trying to do so. He seems to live for the exuberance of the moment." Fender, who thought the 20-year-old "brilliant, if unsound", did not think he would succeed in England. It was a bit like someone watching The Beatles in their early days at the Cavern Club in Liverpool and forecasting that they wouldn't go on to crack America. Don Bradman didn't just succeed on his first trip to England in 1930, he enjoyed the most prolific series of anyone in history. By the time it was done he'd scored 974 runs at 139.14 and shoved Fender's words so far down his throat that they practically had to be surgically removed.

The signs were there in the first game in Worcester. Bradman scored 236, starting a love affair with the ground that continued with innings of 206 in 1934, 258 in 1938 and

107 on his valedictory visit in 1948. In total, Bradman scored 807 runs in four innings at New Road at an average of 201.75. He was a serial killer in front of the cathedral. In the second match of the 1930 tour, at Aylestone Road, Leicester, Bradman followed up with 185 not out, causing eyes to widen – if they hadn't already – to the fact that here was a freakish talent. But the innings that gave him most pleasure came against Surrey at The Oval in May, when he struck an unbeaten 252 against the side captained by Fender, whose doubts had focused on Bradman's bottom-handed grip, which sometimes gave him a closed bat-face. "The innings doubly pleased me," wrote Bradman, "because it showed Fender and other people that I could play in England, and it also set me up for my first 1,000 runs by the end of May."

Bradman was the first Australian to achieve the feat, which he repeated in 1938. He is the only man to have twice reached a mark that has not been hit since 1988, with chance to do so vastly reduced by the systematic shrinkage of first-class cricket. In 1930, Bradman's chance looked to have gone with his total stuck on 954. On the last day of May, Lord Tennyson, the Hampshire captain, won the toss and chose to bat in the Australians' tour game in South-ampton. Bradman's only hope was for the hosts to be dismissed cheaply, which they were as the diminutive

A vintage cigarette card image of Percy Fender, the Surrey captain, who questioned whether the young Don Bradman would succeed in England.

leg-spinner Clarrie Grimmett took seven for 39 to remove them for 151 by mid-afternoon. Promoted to open from his usual No. 3, and playing his 11th innings of the tour, Bradman had hit 28 of the 46 he needed when rain descended at tea. Although a restart was possible, more rain fell when he reached 39, threatening to leave him seven runs short. However, Tennyson – grandson of the poet Alfred Tennyson – sportingly agreed to carry on until Bradman had raised his 1,000. No sooner had he done so than the players dashed for shelter.

A fortnight later, Bradman scored eight and 131 in the First Test at Trent Bridge, which Australia lost by 93 runs, their only defeat of the summer. In the second Test at Lord's, he played what he always rated his best innings technically, scoring 254 in a seven-wicket win. Bradman's innings was the highest in Test cricket by an Australian (beating Victor Trumper's 214 not out against South Africa at Adelaide in 1911) and the highest in a Test in England (beating Billy Murdoch's old world record 211, a score equalled by Jack Hobbs against South Africa at Lord's in 1924). "Practically without exception every ball went where it was intended to go, even the one from which I was dismissed," wrote Bradman, "but the latter went slightly up in the air, and Percy Chapman with a miraculous piece of work held the catch." Chapman, England's dashing and debonair captain, took it one-handed at cover off Somerset left-arm spinner Jack White. For Bradman, pretty much the one disappointment was that he did not beat "Tip" Foster's Ashes record. "I had hopes of beating R. E. Foster's 287 at Sydney in 1903," he said. "As a Sydney player, I felt it was only fitting that I should take the record back to Sydney, and I believe I would have succeeded but for a wonderful catch." By now, Bradman was being spoken of as the greatest batsman the game had seen, even though he was two months short of his 22nd birthday. Even Fender conceded that the 254 was "as perfect an example of real batting, in its best sense, as anyone could wish to see" and was soon proclaiming Bradman "a genius".

If anyone doubted Bradman's right to be so regarded, those doubts evaporated two weeks later. In the Third Test at Leeds, he beat not only Foster's 287 but also Andy Sandham's 325 – 99 days after Sandham set the new mark. Prior to the match, Bradman spent a few days off in London and attended the Wimbledon tennis finals. Suitably recharged, he drove to Yorkshire where the game was billed as "Bradman v England". Australia were forced into two changes: Bill Ponsford, the great Victorian batsman, had gastritis and New South Wales all-rounder Alan Fairfax was recovering from an operation to remove an abscess. Archie Jackson, a brilliant 20-year-old who died of tuberculosis only three years later, and Ted a'Beckett, a tall fast-medium bowler came into the team. England dropped five players – veteran batsmen Frank Woolley and Patsy Hendren, all-rounder Gubby Allen and spinners Walter Robins and Jack White. The hosts welcomed back Herbert Sutcliffe from injury to open the batting and Harold Larwood from illness to open the bowling.

Larwood, the Nottinghamshire fast bowler, had been struck down by tonsillitis in the First Test closely followed by problems with his teeth and was "still looking very drawn", according to *Wisden*. The Almanack said he "had not the stamina to bowl at his full pace" and was "terribly expensive", going on to return one for 139 from 33 overs and receiving from Bradman "a merciless pasting". However, some 35 years later, Larwood claimed that he should have had Bradman out for a duck. "Even before he had scored I had him caught behind the wicket," he wrote in his autobiography. "There is no doubt in my mind he was palpably out. Everyone around the wicket appealed, even Jack Hobbs, the fairest man I ever met on a cricket field." According to Larwood, it would have left Australia one for two after he'd caught Jackson at short leg off his opening partner Maurice Tate from the 11th ball after Australia captain Bill Woodfull won the toss. Larwood said that he "never moaned about it" at the time because "I've always believed you have to take the rough with the smooth, and the umpire gave his decision". He said that he "expected a man to leave the crease when he was out" and that "any member of the English team, like Wally Hammond, Herbert Sutcliffe or George Duckworth, could confirm the fact that Don snicked the ball but was given the benefit by the umpire". Irving Rosenwater, the former BBC television statistician and Bradman's biographer, contested Larwood's claim, pointing out that he didn't bowl to Bradman before he had scored. "Larwood is certainly mistaken," he wrote. "This alleged incident was at a time when Bradman's arrival at the crease brought almost a ball-by-ball description of his movements in the newspapers, and the entire – and not inconsiderable – press contingent at Headingley seems to have failed to notice the appeal or alternatively to have conspired to suppress it." He added that Larwood's claim "has never been supported by any of the players or the 20,000 spectators present".

According to Neville Cardus, Bradman was guilty of a solitary mis-hit before lunch, flashing a cut past Chapman at point on 36. Otherwise, on an unseasonably cold July day, with the threat of rain never far away, he continued from where he left off at Lord's, pummelling what *The Times* dismissed as "colourless and undistinguished" bowling with an "absence of sting". On an easy-paced pitch scattered with bare spots, the newspaper added that Larwood, 25, who usually operated at 90mph-plus despite a comparatively slender frame, "came off the pitch no faster than was comfortable to the batsmen and scarcely ever made the ball come back". Tate, the genial 35-year-old Sussex pace bowler, "only once or twice could get the ball past the bat", while George Geary, a tall and strong Leicestershire paceman, who'd turned 37 two days earlier, "could do little more than keep the runs down". The attack, completed by rotund Lancashire leg-spinner Dick Tyldesley, 33, with support from batsmen Wally Hammond and Maurice Leyland, laboured in the benign conditions. "The English bowlers bore every appearance of hoping that a batsman would get out, rather than of suspecting that they would get him out," said *The Times*.

Among the watching press corps was Charlie Macartney, one of only two men to have hit a hundred before lunch in a Test at the time. An attacking player nicknamed "The Governor-General", Macartney did so in the corresponding match at Headingley in 1926, equalling the feat of fellow countryman Victor Trumper in the 1902 Manchester Test. Now Bradman joined the exalted company, reaching his hundred at Headingley with 13 minutes to spare – the same margin as Macartney – and going on to 105 out of 136 for one at lunch. Woodfull, the tortoise to Bradman's hare, batted through the session for 29 as England – in stark contrast to today's soporific trends – sent down 46 overs.

Helped by the healthy over-rate, Bradman sprinted to his double-hundred just before tea in the dizzying time of 214

Bradman on his way to the new Test record.

minutes. It was 20 minutes faster than his double at Lord's, his only aberrations coming on 141 and 202 when he twice skyed towards mid-on where no one was swift enough to take the chance. Otherwise, with Woodfull the only casualty of the middle session, bowled by Hammond for 50 after adding 192 with Bradman, the prodigy played every shot going. "To mention the strokes from which he scored most of his runs is to go through the whole range of strokes known to a modern batsman," said *The Times*. "Once or twice he demonstrated an idea which is not generally understood, but at no time did he take anything approaching a risk, and he cannot have hit the ball in the air more than three times during the day. It was, in fact, an innings so glorious that it might well be classed as incomparable, and how the Yorkshiremen loved it." At tea, Bradman had 220 out of 305 for two, his graceful New South Wales team-mate Alan Kippax on 33.

According to the *Daily Telegraph*, Bradman scored his runs with "an almost imperceptible twist of his bat", reaching the boundary "by strikingly different routes". His method, by no means culled from the coaching book, had been honed in his boyhood in Bowral, a country town some 70 miles south-west of Sydney. Bradman would throw a golf ball against the brick base of a water tank at the family home and strike it with a cricket stump as it rebounded at different angles and speeds. Although he didn't realise it then, he was developing his reflexes and rubberlike wrists.

Five feet seven and physically slight, Bradman – a carpenter's son and the youngest of five children – used a light bat that weighed between 2lb 2oz and 2lb 4oz. He believed that footwork was the key to good batting, saying: "It is to batting what a foundation is to a house. Without it there can be no structure." Bradman seemed to move into position quicker than others and hit the ball powerfully off the back foot particularly, his feet as nimble as Fred Astaire. What set him apart, however, was his concentration; he was machine-like in how he churned out runs. R. C. Robertson-Glasgow called him "that rarest of Nature's creations, an artist without the handicap of the artistic temperament, a genius with an eye to business", while the *Yorkshire Post* correspondent J. M. Kilburn described him as "a textbook of batting come to life with never a misprint or erratum". Larwood found Bradman "calculating and assured" and said there was "no answer" to him in 1930. "Don was cruel the way he flogged you," he added. "He seemed to have a computer-type approach, never giving anything away and always able to go his own inexorable way. He jumped down the pitch to the bowlers just when he felt like it, which was most of the time." Jack Hobbs thought Bradman "too good" to the point that he "spoilt the game". "I do not think we want to see another one quite like him," he said, adding: "I do not think we ever will."

Such was Bradman's determination, *Wisden* said "he could be 250 not out and yet still scampering the first run to third man or long leg with a view to inducing a fielding error". Loud cheers resounded at Headingley when Bradman reached that milestone in the final session for the second time in consecutive Tests. There were further cheers when he went past his Lord's total of 254 to be replaced by a nervous, expectant hush as he closed in on Foster's 287. Bradman almost fell agonisingly short; just before six o'clock, with his score standing at 273, he gave his only chance – Duckworth dropping a difficult catch behind the stumps off Geary. By now, Bradman's runs had dried to a trickle, his earlier carefree progress replaced by a crawl. But after inching up to 283, he hooked Tate to the fine-leg boundary to draw level with Foster and followed that with a hooked single off Tate to lift him to 288. The match came to a joyous standstill as Headingley proclaimed the hero of the hour. "The enthusiasm was unbounded," wrote the *Daily Telegraph*, "and the game was held up for fully a couple of minutes so that the cheers might be prolonged. He [Bradman] waved his hand to express his joy, and for the first time indulged in a happy and expansive smile." According to *The Times*: "No ground in the world, not even his own Sydney, could have offered him such sincere and prolonged congratulations as did the crowd at Leeds."

Tellingly, both newspapers – in common with their English and Australian counterparts – said that Bradman had achieved the highest individual score in Test cricket. There was no mention whatsoever of Sandham's 325, as if, like the

What a feeling: Bradman acknowledges the Headingley crowd after passing "Tip" Foster's Ashes record.

atheist view of God, it didn't exist. The only Tests that counted in the eyes of press and public continued to be those involving England, Australia and South Africa. Perhaps if Sandham's record had stayed a bit longer, instead of being erased almost before his sore feet had healed, it would have burrowed more deeply into the public consciousness as Test cricket expanded across the globe. As it was, it effectively went in one ear and out of the other, and if ever there was a bad time to set a new Test batting record, it was surely in the spring of 1930 ahead of Bradman's phenomenal summer. "If Foster's record had to be beaten it was an innings which was a fitting one to take its place, and no praise could be higher," wrote Percy Fender. The man once sceptical of Bradman's ability to thrive in England was particularly taken with his style of hooking. "Bradman established for all time a new method of hooking," he said. "It is not new to him, but it is to cricket in general, for no one else uses it, or ever has. Many batsmen hook, but they make the stroke upwards, or, at best, horizontally, while Bradman has shown that the best method is to hook very definitely downwards. That shot will be learned and copied by many, and is a safer, and more lucrative stroke than the old one."

Also writing on this Test was Plum Warner, "Tip" Foster's captain in 1903. Of Bradman, who'd been batting for five and a half hours when he passed Foster, whose own innings lasted some 90 minutes longer, he said: "There has never been a batsman who, in match after match, has claimed such a huge proportion of the runs scored. You may talk of Alexander the Great, Hercules, Trumper and Macartney, but this young Australian is a super-batsman and the equal of anyone."

Barely had the applause ceased for Bradman's Ashes record when Kippax, the 33-year-old right-hander, was brilliantly caught by Chapman at backward point off Tate, leaving Australia 423 for three. The third-wicket pair added 229, Bradman going on to 309 out of 458 for three at stumps on day one (309 was the same number of runs that it took Sandham two days to make against the West Indies). Such was the rush to congratulate Bradman, with spectators swarming the pavilion entrance, that police had to help him off the field. Afterwards, it was said that he was too shy to appear before the lingering throngs, preferring to sip tea in the privacy of the dressing-room. Bradman, whose last scoring shot for the day took him to 2,000 runs for the season, allegedly told captain Woodfull: "That wasn't a bad bit of practice. I'll be able to have a go at them tomorrow." Later, talking to reporters, he said in his distinctive, high-pitched voice: "My feet are awfully tired, but I could have gone on if it hadn't been the close. I am happy to have beaten the record, but happier still to think that Australia is in such a good position."

Bradman returned to the team hotel in the centre of Leeds, where his fellow players wanted to celebrate with him. However, the maestro desired to stay in his room, writing letters and listening to music. In those days, cricket was a much more social game, but Bradman was never a social animal. He said that such functions were not to his taste and limited them "as far as was consistent with decency". "Was I expected to parade the streets of Leeds?" he protested in his autobiography, adding that he "did not think it my duty to breast the bar and engage in a beer-drinking contest". Such off-field discipline and self-control – mirroring that which he showed on the field – made him unpopular with some of his peers. "A solitary man with a solitary aim," was R. C. Robertson-Glasgow's summary of Bradman, who instead of living it up in the bar quietly updated his personal diary.

> "Archie [Jackson] out for 1. I followed and at stumps was 309 not out, breaking the previous highest score in Anglo-Australian Tests. Reached my 2,000 runs for the season. To hotel in evening for dinner and wrote letters, thence to bed."

Bradman was criticised later in the match for not throwing a team meal despite being given £1,000 to honour his feat. The gift from Arthur Whitelaw, an Australian businessman who'd gone to England and made a fortune in soap manufacturing, was £400 more than any Australian player's tour fee and worth about £50,000 today. Bradman was said to have told his colleagues: "If I gave you fellows a dinner every night from now until we get home to Australia, you would only say what a fool I am." Jack Fingleton, a future international team-mate, claimed that if Bradman had so much as bought a round of drinks, "many would not have had one", while another future international team-mate, Bill O'Reilly, famously said that "the Bradman Appreciation Society held its meetings in a telephone kiosk".

For all that Bradman was an acquired taste among colleagues, some of whom were no doubt jealous, he was worshipped by the man in the street. In Australia he became a symbol of hope for a hopeless Joe Public, struggling to survive in the Great Depression. At the time of his innings, almost one-third of Australia's workforce was unemployed, and Bradman answered the need for a hero. He provided escape from the mundane misery of day-to-day life and some lived their dreams through his cricketing exploits. Bradman's rise also coincided with the spread of radio and cinema newsreels. People could follow his success and share in it too. Australia craved a culture and an identity separate from Britain, a stronger footing on the map of Empire. Bradman was not just a standard-bearer for Australian cricket, but for Australia.

Many Englishmen wished that he'd never left the place – not least the anonymous wag who sent him a telegram on day two at Headingley. Bradman was about to resume his innings when the following message was pushed in his palm: "Your house is on fire and your girl wants you back – go home." Another English fan suggested a "Fund for the Assassination of Bradman". The man took it in good spirits but no doubt used it as extra spur.

Day two, a Saturday, was bright and breezy, and after adding 28 runs to their overnight score, Australia lost two quick wickets. Larwood knocked down the leg stump of New South Wales batsman Stan McCabe, who was four days short of his 20th birthday. Then, fielding at short leg to Tate, Larwood caught Vic Richardson, a brilliant all-round sportsman and grandfather of the Chappell brothers – Ian, Greg and Trevor. Moments later, to "a roar which could have been heard in Sheffield", Bradman was dismissed for 334. He tried to drive Tate past mid-on but edged to wicketkeeper Duckworth standing up to the stumps. Before that misjudgement, Cardus wrote that Bradman "reminded me of the trapeze performer who one night decided to commit suicide by flinging himself headlong to the stage, but could not achieve the error because his skill had become infallible". Bradman exited to a standing ovation, dark suits and trilbies rising as one. The ground, then shaded by elms at the Kirkstall Lane end, and surrounded by a concrete cycle track, was still echoing long after the wunderkind disappeared from view.

Bradman's innings lasted 383 minutes and spanned 448 balls. It contained 46 fours, six threes, 26 twos and 80 singles. Having started the year with 452 not out for New South Wales against Queensland at Sydney, which beat the previous first-class record of 437 by Bill Ponsford for Victoria against Queensland at Melbourne a little over two years earlier, Bradman now held the highest Test and first-class scores simultaneously – something not repeated until Brian Lara first did it in 1994. The 334 just failed to beat the highest score by an Australian in England (Charlie Macartney's 345 against Nottinghamshire at Trent Bridge in 1921) and it remained the highest score in a first-class match at Headingley

Bradman is welcomed in after his 334.

until another Australian, Darren Lehmann, hit 339 on his final appearance for Yorkshire, against Durham in 2006. Although he later denied it, Lehmann seemed to throw his wicket away deliberately to ensure that the Yorkshire record of 341 stayed with local legend George Hirst.

From 486 for three when McCabe was out, Australia collapsed to 566. They dismissed England for 391 (Hammond collecting a hundred and Grimmett five wickets) and had them 95 for three in the follow-on when rain and bad light had the final word. Having more than doubled the bar set by Charles Bannerman with his 165 in the inaugural Test, Bradman added another double-century (232) in the final match at The Oval to give Australia an innings win and the series 2–1. It exacted revenge for a 4–1 thumping in the previous Ashes series in 1928-29 and meant that the ten Ashes campaigns since "Tip" Foster's 287 had been shared at five apiece. Bradman scored another triple-century at Leeds in 1934 (304), hit 103 and 16 in the 1938 Leeds Test and, in the 1948 Ashes match there, struck 33 and 173 not out, helping Australia to a Test-record chase of 404 and a seven-wicket triumph. In four Tests and six innings at Leeds, Bradman scored 963 runs at an average of 192.60. In recognition, Yorkshire CCC made him its first honorary overseas life member, tantamount to making him an honorary Yorkshireman.

After Bradman's exploits in 1930, debate raged as to how his brilliance could possibly be dimmed. Some suggested he be made to play with a smaller bat, as was once said of W. G. Grace, while others felt that the legendary Sydney Barnes, now 57 but still playing for Staffordshire, should be recalled to teach him a lesson. The *Daily Telegraph* called Bradman

The Australian squad in 1930. Standing (l–r): Stan McCabe, Alec Hurwood, Tim Wall, Percy Hornibrook, Ted A'Beckett, Alan Kippax, Clarrie Grimmett, Bert Oldfield. Sitting (l–r): Don Bradman, Bill Ponsford, Victor Richardson, Bill Woodfull (captain), Charlie Walker, Archie Jackson, Alan Fairfax.

"a whole team in himself", adding that "if there is room for wonder, it is that he is ever out". The *Daily Express* said "he will soon have to be handicapped, as are billiards players, before he starts to score" and that "it is either compelling him to owe 100 or blindfolding him that will stop his gallop". As it turned out, the man who best worked out how to stop him, or at least to slow him, was Douglas Jardine, captain for the return Ashes series in 1932-33. In the final Test at The Oval in 1930, Jardine noticed that Bradman flinched and retreated to leg against rising balls from Larwood on a wicket spiced by rain. The tall and authoritative Surrey batsman, with aquiline features and acid demeanour, concluded that Bradman was "yellow" and used the twin pace-bowling spearheads of Larwood and Bill Voce in an effort to prove it. They peppered him and his Australian team-mates with short balls into the body with a packed leg-side field, a terrifying tactic in the pre-helmet era. As England swept to a 4–1 win, Bradman was chopped to around half-size – averaging 56.57 compared to an overall Test average of 99.94. That England were so scared of him that they devised a whole new method of bowling – popularly known as Bodyline – was tribute to the greatest phenomenon the game has seen. To this day, the fairness of Bodyline divides opinion as surely as whether a civilised society should allow the death penalty.

Bodyline excepted, Bradman's career proceeded in unmitigated triumph. One could fill an entire book with his statistical achievements and still have room for follow-up volumes. Had he scored four runs in his last Test innings at The Oval in 1948, when Warwickshire leg-spinner Eric Hollies bowled him for a second-ball duck, Bradman would have averaged exactly 100 in Tests. As it was, the 99.94 kept him just on the human side of divine and made him roughly one-third better than anyone else statistically, something never satisfactorily explained. Bradman hit 29 hundreds in 52 Tests, 117 in 234 first-class games and would have put more beads on the groaning abacus but for the Second World War, which took out most of his thirties. He was later a selector and administrator and was knighted for his services to cricket in 1949. Only W. G. Grace has remotely matched his status in the sport and, like Grace, he transcended sport. When he died in February 2001, aged 92, it was one of the rare occasions that Bradman did not reach a century.

Such was his fame in that storied summer of 1930, newspaper sellers carried placards which simply said "He's Out!", with no further explanation needed. Bradman finished the tour with 2,960 runs in all first-class matches at an average of 98.66, with ten three-figure scores in 27 appearances. Summing up the Australians' trip, Irving Rosenwater wrote: "Though 11 cricketers appeared in every side Bradman played for, and though Grimmett took 29 wickets in the Test series (and 144 on the tour) and Woodfull's captaincy was immaculate throughout, all eyes and pens were firmly focused on the Sydney marvel, with the rest of the players satellites revolving around the sun." R. C. Robertson-Glasgow said that Bradman "did not mean to be just one of the stars, but the sun itself".

When the sun set on Bradman's glorious career, he remembered no happier occasion than the 1930 Headingley Test. "I consider I was very lucky to strike my best form on an ideal batsman's wicket," he said, adding that "the opening day of the Third Test at Leeds must rank as the greatest of my cricketing life".

England v Australia

Played at Headingley, Leeds, on 11, 12, 14, 15 July, 1930.

Toss: Australia. Result: Match drawn.

AUSTRALIA

*W. M. Woodfull b Hammond	50	C. V. Grimmett c Duckworth b Tyldesley			24
A. Jackson c Larwood b Tate	1	T. W. Wall b Tyldesley			3
D. G. Bradman c Duckworth b Tate	334	P. M. Hornibrook not out			1
A. F. Kippax c Chapman b Tate	77	B 5, lb 8, w 1			14
S. J. McCabe b Larwood	30				
V. Y. Richardson c Larwood b Tate	1	1/2 (2) 2/194 (1) 3/423 (4)		(168 overs)	566
E. L. a'Beckett c Chapman b Geary	29	4/486 (5) 5/491 (6) 6/508 (3)			
†W. A. S. Oldfield c Hobbs b Tate	2	7/519 (8) 8/544 (7) 9/565 (10) 10/566 (9)			

Larwood 33-3-139-1; Tate 39-9-124-5; Geary 35-10-95-1; Tyldesley 33-5-104-2;
Hammond 17-3-46-1; Leyland 11-0-44-0.

ENGLAND

J. B. Hobbs c a'Beckett b Grimmett	29	– run out (Bradman/Oldfield)		13
H. Sutcliffe c Hornibrook b Grimmett	32	– not out		28
W. R. Hammond c Oldfield b McCabe	113	– c Oldfield b Grimmett		35
K. S. Duleepsinhji b Hornibrook	35	– c Grimmett b Hornibrook		10
M. Leyland c Kippax b Wall	44	– not out		1
G. Geary run out (Wall/Oldfield)	0			
†G. Duckworth c Oldfield b a'Beckett	33			
*A. P. F. Chapman b Grimmett	45			
M. W. Tate c Jackson b Grimmett	22			
H. Larwood not out	10			
R. K. Tyldesley c Hornibrook b Grimmett	6			
B 9, lb 10, nb 3	22	Lb 8		8

1/53 (1) 2/64 (2) 3/123 (4)   (175.2 overs) 391   1/24 (1)   (3 wkts, 51.5 overs) 95
4/206 (5) 5/206 (6) 6/289 (7)   2/72 (3) 3/94 (4)
7/319 (3) 8/370 (8) 9/375 (9) 10/391 (11)

Wall 40-12-70-1; a'Beckett 28-8-47-1; Grimmett 56.2-16-135-5; Hornibrook 41-7-94-1;
McCabe 10-4-23-1. *Second innings* — Wall 10-3-20-0; a'Beckett 11-4-19-0;
Grimmett 17-3-33-1; Hornibrook 11.5-5-14-1; McCabe 2-1-1-0.

Umpires: W. Bestwick and T. W. Oates.

6

Wally Hammond (336*)
England versus New Zealand
Auckland 1933

After the fire and fury of Bodyline, when Don Bradman was briefly reduced to mortal, England travelled to New Zealand for a contrastingly cordial two-Test series. It was a bit like a weather forecast at the end of a dramatic news bulletin, an incongruous postscript mostly forgotten. A greater contrast to the baying and barracking of Australian crowds – distant echoes across the Tasman – would have been difficult to conceive for Douglas Jardine and his touring party. It was a party shorn of Harold Larwood, who'd gone home injured after the Fifth and final Test at Sydney. Jardine bowled him into the parched Australian earth to the extent that he severely damaged his left big toe and was never the same again. Jardine's desire to crush Bradman was such that he refused to allow the lame Larwood to leave the field at the SCG until Bradman was out in the second innings, despite the fact that the series was won. When Larwood broke down in mid-over, Jardine firstly made him finish it and then ordered him to field at cover – the pretence being that Larwood was suffering from cramp and could soon return for another spell. Only when Hedley Verity bowled Bradman with his left-arm spin did Jardine relent, Larwood and Bradman exiting together without exchanging looks or words.

With neither its principal perpetrator nor target around, there was no Bodyline bowling in New Zealand. The series was played in fine spirit and with happy fellowship off the field. For different reasons both sides wanted to show that they preferred each other's company to that of Australians, with the Australian Board of Control having opposed this appendix to the Ashes tour. Jardine considered its stance unacceptable and believed it stemmed from Australia's contempt for the emerging prowess of New Zealand, then in its fourth year as an active Test nation. So deep was Jardine's dislike of Australians, which practically bordered on religious zeal, he never missed a chance to decry them in public speeches or private conversation. Jardine also kept banging on about Australia's flies, as if they'd followed him across the Tasman. While staying with relatives of the former England captain Percy Chapman, who'd married the sister of the New Zealand cricketer Tom Lowry, Jardine was even said to have "evinced symptoms of acute paranoia" in those early weeks after Bodyline. Fearing that he might be assassinated at any moment, he insisted on keeping the back door open in case he had to make a getaway.

On arrival in New Zealand, Jardine and his players were greeted by Prime Minister George Forbes at a reception at Wellington Town Hall. Perhaps with a mocking nod to their Antipodean brethren, the band struck up "See the Conquering Hero Comes". It was just one example of the hospitality and kindness extended to the tourists, with the players practically treated like gods. From Maori welcomes to touching farewells, they were feted like royalty wherever they went. The tour consisted of eight days' cricket with a two-day warm-up against Wellington followed by three-day Tests in Christchurch and Auckland.

The first day of the Wellington match was washed out, 16,000 then filling the ground on the final day to see MCC score 223 for eight declared, Wellington reaching 141 for two in reply. Wally Hammond top-scored with 58 for the tourists despite a septic knee that meant he had to bat with a runner. The night ferry then took the England players to Christchurch where, two days later, the First Test started at Lancaster Park.

Hammond had come to New Zealand in splendid form. The Gloucestershire star – three months short of his 30th birthday – had no superior then apart from Bradman. Hammond had joint top-scored in the Bodyline series along with England team-mate Herbert Sutcliffe, the pair boasting an identical record of 440 runs at an average of 55. It was 44 runs more than Bradman made, although he played in only four of the five Tests and had a slightly better average. Hammond was the only man to score two hundreds in the series: 112 in the First Test at Sydney (the match that Bradman missed due to feeling run down) and 101 in the final game at the same venue. In the second innings of that last Test, Hammond's unbeaten 75 included a match-winning six off spinner "Perker" Lee, an emphatic end to a stormy series. Years later, Hammond revealed that he disapproved of Bodyline, a stance intensified when he faced a barrage of short stuff from the West Indies in 1933 and had his chin split open. As well as his runs in the Bodyline campaign, Hammond scored 203 against Victoria and 101 against Queensland Country. If not quite a repeat of his form on the previous Ashes tour, when his total of 905 Test runs was a record until Bradman's 974 in 1930, he remained England's best batsman in a line going back to W. G. Grace.

Although equally synonymous with the "Glorious Glosters", whom he represented from 1920 to 1946 (plus a solitary appearance in 1951), Hammond was born in Buckland, Kent, on the outskirts of Dover in 1903. His father, William, was a bombardier stationed at Dover Castle, whose overseas postings saw the young Hammond spend three years living in Hong Kong followed by another three living in Malta. When the family returned to England, Hammond was sent to Portsmouth Grammar School and then – for reasons never elucidated – to board at Cirencester Grammar School in Gloucestershire. He'd not been there long when the sad news came through that his father had been killed in action in the First World War. Hammond's cricket shone at the school and the headmaster recommended him to Gloucestershire. They handed him his first-class debut at the 1920 Cheltenham Festival, two months after his 17th birthday. Hammond played infrequently during the next two years, the Kent chairman Lord Harris – piqued that he was not representing his native county – having kicked up a fuss at Lord's. Harris, the England captain when Billy Murdoch beat Charles Bannerman's score, was a pedantic stickler for the letter of the law, which then said that a player could only qualify for another county by living there for at least two years. Hammond was made to bide his time. "I was livid," he said, "and I was also perfectly helpless."

In those earliest days, Hammond also played professional football. He spent three seasons as a winger with Bristol Rovers, making 20 appearances and scoring twice. Some thought that Hammond had the talent to play football for England as well as cricket, à la "Tip" Foster. However, he never showed much enthusiasm for the winter game and was cautious going in for tackles, fearing that injury could affect his main forte. Instead, it was serious illness – as opposed to any injury playing in the lower reaches of the Third Division South – which, for a time, threatened not only Hammond's cricketing career but also his life. During MCC's tour of West Indies in 1925-26, which comprised 12 first-class games against the colonies and representative XIs, Hammond fell desperately ill. He attributed it to a mosquito bite in the groin area near to a pre-existing muscle strain, leading to blood poisoning. However, David Foot, the former *Guardian* cricket writer and Hammond's biographer, who consulted many medical experts in the course of his research, concluded that Hammond actually contracted "a form of

Wally Hammond, third from left on the middle row, with the MCC team in the West Indies in 1926. Hammond fell desperately ill during the tour and almost died. Freddie Calthorpe, the England captain when Andy Sandham took the record, is fourth from the left on the front row.

syphilis or a related sexually transmitted disease". The young Hammond underwent 12 operations of essentially experimental treatment to find out what was wrong with him, which, said Foot, only "added to the tortures and uncertainties of his protracted recovery". Hammond missed the entire 1926 English season and said: "I understand they'd almost given me up for dead."

When he returned in 1927, the reason for his absence shrouded in secrecy, Hammond revealed the extent of his genius. In 13 innings between May 7 and May 28 he became only the third player after W. G. Grace and Tom Hayward to score 1,000 first-class runs by the end of May, recording five centuries and an innings of 99. Hammond ended that season with just under 3,000 runs at an average slightly below 70, the start of a sequence in which he scored more than 2,000 runs in five of the six English seasons leading into the 1932-33 Australasian tour.

In one particularly astonishing week at Cheltenham in 1928, when Gloucestershire played Surrey and Worcestershire, Hammond proved himself not only a great batsman but also the greatest all-rounder of the day. He began by scoring a hundred in each innings against Surrey, taking ten catches in the match at his usual first-slip position, and bowling Jack Hobbs with his brand of medium-fast cutters and swingers delivered with a perfect side-on action. Six foot tall and built like a heavyweight, Hammond then captured a career-best nine for 23 against Worcestershire (he caught the other batsman), took six second innings wickets and hit 80 on his solitary visit to the crease. Across those five days at the picturesque College Ground, shaded by the watching Cotswolds, Hammond scored 362 runs, claimed 16 wickets and held 11 catches. Had he not been such a reluctant bowler à la Jacques Kallis, the South African who ranks with him in the pantheon of all-rounders, Hammond would have been remembered more for his all-round skills instead of his primary brilliance as a batsman.

It was a brilliance that blinded New Zealand in 1933 when Hammond broke Bradman's record for the highest Test score. *Wisden* described the tour as "a valuable missionary move", highlighting the somewhat condescending attitude prevalent at the time and the context in which the series was played. Ever since Harold Gilligan's side had toured there in early 1930, when England played two Tests on opposite sides of the world simultaneously, New Zealand had made encouraging strides in Test cricket, albeit were still seeking their first Test win. They'd played three Tests in England in 1931, showing such form in a draw at Lord's – the only originally scheduled game – that a further two were arranged. Hammond scored an unbeaten century in the first of them, an innings victory at The Oval, before the Manchester Test was ruined by the weather. The opening Test of the 1933 series in Christchurch was only New Zealand's tenth Test match and their first against a fully representative England team.

Hammond warmed up for his record-breaking performance to come with an innings of 227, despite not having fully recovered from his septic knee. Proceedings began sensationally when Herbert Sutcliffe was caught behind off the first ball of the match after Douglas Jardine won the toss. Fellow opener Eddie Paynter also fell for a duck to the first ball of the second over. In between times, Hammond was dropped in the slips – a miss that *Wisden* said was "typical of New Zealand's faulty fielding". Hammond's innings lifted England to 560 for eight declared, New Zealand replying with 223. The hosts were 35 for nought following on when a violent dust storm – followed by rain and bad light – dramatically ended the Test. Hammond remembered how, "with amazing suddenness, there arose such a screaming hurricane of wind that cricket became literally impossible".

Prior to the Second and last Test in Auckland, Hammond and his colleagues enjoyed a sightseeing trip around North Island. They visited the hot springs of Rotorua – Jardine stayed on there to nurse a bout of rheumatism, with Bob Wyatt captaining the side at Eden Park – and they marvelled at the lakes and snow-capped mountains. Herbert Sutcliffe described New Zealand as "a jewel of a country", while his Yorkshire team-mate Bill Bowes, the tall and bespectacled pace bowler, said that "after England, New Zealand is the finest land in the world". After six scorched months in Australia, the players were thrilled by the fresh green countryside and its soothing echoes of faraway home.

During this four-day interval between Tests, Hammond went sword-fishing as a guest of Bay of Islands Fishing Club. He described these fish as "the Nazis of the oceans" as they "attack not only sharks and whales, but even ships, apparently in moods of wanton aggression". Hammond called the Pacific sharks "terrific fellows, 70 feet and more in length" but added that "certainly none of us wanted to have any arguments with them". Summing up his experiences, he said: "Sailing the blue bays off New Zealand, with the glorious mountains and glaciers in the distance, and the prospect of fun and excitement with the big fish, is a pastime of which I should never tire."

The Auckland Test should have started on April Fool's Day but was brought forward 24 hours so that England could

Hammond in action.

catch an earlier boat home. Curly Page, the New Zealand captain and a former All Blacks scrum-half, won the toss and saw his side dismissed for 158, Bowes returning six for 34 and Stewie Dempster, a neat and compact right-hander, top-scoring with 83 not out. In glorious weather, before around 5,000 people, Hammond came in at No. 3 after Sutcliffe slapped a long-hop to cover, ending an opening stand of 56 with Wyatt. Hammond's walk to the wicket was one of the great sights of cricket, not unlike that of Viv Richards in modern times. "He came like a king and he looked like a king in his coming," wrote J. M. Kilburn, who said that Hammond "could never be seen without being remembered" and that, "in his time, a Test match could not seem a Test match in his absence". *Wisden* wrote of the Hammond entrance: "The instant he walked out of a pavilion, white-spotted blue handkerchief showing from his right pocket, bat tucked underarm, cap at a hint of an angle, he was identifiable as a thoroughbred. Strongly-built, square-shouldered, deep-chested, with impressively powerful forearms, it seemed as if his bat weighed nothing in those purposeful hands."

According to the Press Association, the only mainstream outlet present as those which had staffed the Ashes had not bothered with these games, Hammond began his innings with "effortless ease". He was particularly strong on the leg side en route to 41 at stumps, reached in 57 minutes with six fours. At the other end, Wyatt made 56 out of 127 for one, play ending 50 minutes early when Wyatt complained that the setting sun was in his eyes. More glorious weather favoured day two, Wyatt adding four runs to his overnight score before off-spinner Jack Dunning bowled him. Hammond knocked off the nine he required for his half-century and then suddenly started to "go for the bowling", establishing "an absolute mastery over the attack of Dunning, Badcock, Newman and Freeman, with no bowler escaping punishment".

It was an attack led by all-rounder Ted Badcock, a 35-year-old right-arm pace bowler and aggressive batsman. Dunning, 30, with whom he shared the new ball, could bowl fast-ish medium in addition to spin. Jack Newman, also 30, was a left-arm medium-pacer and Doug Freeman a 6ft 3in leg-spinner. At 18 years and 197 days, Freeman was New Zealand's youngest Test cricketer until fellow spinner Daniel Vettori (18 years and ten days) against England at Wellington in 1997. Freeman had chutzpah to match his height and recalled having a set-to with Wyatt during this game.

Noticing that the England captain was backing up too far, Freeman asked: "Excuse me, Mr Wyatt, but are you leaving your crease before I have bowled?" Wyatt apologised but carried on anyway. "I shudder to think of the outcry if I had taken off the bails and run him out."

None of which discomfited Hammond, who raced on to a sparkling century, reached with a straight-driven six off Dunning. He'd hit ten fours to go with the six and had been batting for two and a quarter hours. Hammond "continued to hit with glorious freedom" before giving the first of three chances. On 134, he hammered a ball from Freeman to mid-off where Dunning made "a valiant but unsuccessful attempt to take a hot drive". Hammond was dropped by Dempster off another fierce drive, this time off Badcock, who then failed to hold a rasping return. Reports made no mention of Hammond's scores on the last two occasions but Dempster and Badcock were forced off for running repairs. Hammond's strokeplay was famously savage, R. C. Robertson-Glasgow saying that "to field to him at cover point was a sort of ordeal by fire". He added that Hammond possessed "a combined power and grace that I have never seen in any other man" and called him "the sort of cricketer that any schoolboy might want to be". Hammond reached his 150 just before lunch, his third half-century arriving in 37 minutes. England's lunchtime score was 282 for two, an ominous lead of 124.

As news of Hammond's performance spread, the crowd expanded to 15,000. An old newspaper cutting shows a line of people standing beside the boundary fence, which stretched halfway around Eden Park, with a cycle track separating them from the mass of a crowd that rose up behind them. Among that crowd was nine-year-old Bert

"The sort of cricketer that any schoolboy might want to be" – R. C. Robertson-Glasgow's description of Hammond, surrounded here by awestruck youngsters.

Sutcliffe, who grew up to become one of New Zealand's best batsmen. On his Test debut against England at Christchurch in 1947, Sutcliffe caught Hammond in Hammond's last Test innings. Following his regal walk to the wicket that time, Hammond received three cheers from the New Zealand fielders and the crowd sang "For he's a jolly good fellow". He touched his cap in gratitude and bowed out with 79 in a rain-ruined game.

As the schoolboy Sutcliffe looked on in Auckland, Hammond "went on flogging the bowling". He lost Eddie Paynter with the score on 288 – the Lancashire left-hander contributing 36 to their third-wicket stand of 149 – and Kent's Les Ames with the total on 347, bowled around his legs by Badcock. After lofting Freeman for another straight six, Hammond reached his double-century in four hours and celebrated with three successive off-side sixes off Newman. PA said that Hammond was "playing with almost reckless abandon", adding that "the crowd was galvanised into excitement and cheer after cheer went up as Hammond proceeded to bash the bowling all round the ground". Gubby Allen, the 30-year-old Middlesex all-rounder, was also bowled around his legs by Badcock, and Freddie Brown, the 22-year-old Surrey all-rounder, sixth out at 456 when skying to cover. "But this did not worry Hammond," said PA, "who continued to pierce the field as he pleased". Two more offside sixes off Badcock took Hammond past his previous Test-best of 251 against Australia at Sydney in 1928, when he'd missed the chance to beat "Tip" Foster. But there was no passing up that prospect now; Hammond sailed past Foster's 287 and closed in fast on his triple-hundred, the crowd urging him on his historic way.

It was at this point, however, that Hammond broke his trusty light bat. He didn't have any spares with him so, just like Andy Sandham in 1930, he borrowed from a team-mate – the Derbyshire leg-spinner Tommy Mitchell, a proverbial No. 11 whose bats got scant use during a career in which he averaged 7.97. "It is a little difficult to start work with a new bat when a record is being approached," wrote Hammond, "but the new one settled into my hands as well as the old." Bill Voce, the Nottinghamshire pace bowler – who, along with Wyatt and Ames, played in Sandham's game – was bowled on the stroke of tea, at which point the score was 506 for seven (Hammond 302). He'd raced from 200 to 300 in 47 minutes – including the delay to change his bat – and Bradman's record was now in sight. On reaching 300, Hammond had also passed the highest Test score since Bradman's 334 – Bradman's own 299 not out against South

Africa at Adelaide in 1932. Bradman ran out the last man "Pud" Thurlow in a desperate effort to keep the strike. "The crowd was now on tiptoes watching Hammond's efforts to beat Bradman's 334," said PA. "As he neared the record, Hammond played with infinite caution."

Hammond later said that he felt supremely confident as history beckoned – "that day, I felt I could do anything". However, he admitted: "All the same, I began to feel 'stage fright' as my score crept up – 320, 325, 330. And then, at last, 334. I had tied Don Bradman. No use hesitating at that stage – and off the very next ball, I yelled: 'Yes!' and we sneaked a wickedly swift single."

According to PA, there was "a tornado of cheers and clapping" as Auckland acclaimed Hammond's achievement. He sported a smile as wide as the Tasman, removed his cap and brandished his bat. Off the very next ball, Hammond was caught, driving Badcock firmly to mid-off. Further cheers resounded, however, when a no-ball was signalled. "I mopped my brow," wrote Hammond. "The excitement was getting too much. But I managed to run another single to make my record sure."

At the end of the over, with Hammond 336 out of 548 for seven, Wyatt declared after first gaining confirmation from the scorers that Hammond had indeed broken the record. Verification was deemed necessary as, during the previous English summer, there had been great controversy when the Yorkshire openers Percy Holmes and Herbert Sutcliffe had broken the world record for the highest stand in first-class cricket. No sooner had they raised 555 against Essex at Leyton than the scorers dramatically reduced the total to 554 – the previous record – when Sutcliffe was out. Amid pandemonium in front of the scorebox, the matter was only resolved when "a reverend gentleman" appeared from the crowd and displayed his own meticulously kept scorebook, which showed 555. A "missing" no-ball was prudently inserted into the official records, Holmes describing the affair as "a rare to-do" and Sutcliffe recoiling in horror at mere mention of the episode until his death over 45 years later.

Hammond's innings contained 34 fours and ten sixes (eight on the off-side, two on the on), a Test record until Wasim Akram hit 12 for Pakistan against Zimbabwe at Sheikhupura in 1996. Although there is no record of how many balls Hammond faced, it has been estimated at 355. His innings spanned five hours, 18 minutes – only 17 minutes longer than he'd batted for his 227 in Christchurch. "It just happened to be my day," he wrote. "The ball looked big in the first over, and got bigger. The field seemed full of gaps where shots could be placed."

Trailing by 390 when they started their second innings deep into the final session on day two, New Zealand had reached eight for nought at stumps. They advanced to 16 for nought on a final day on which rain permitted just 12 minutes' play. PA said there were more seagulls in the ground than spectators, conditions being so wet that Hammond "slipped in the mud when he delivered his first ball". The match was drawn, the series ending 0–0 as Hammond emerged with the extraordinary average of 563 for once out. In the entire Australasian tour, he scored 1,763 runs at 83.95 (the next-best was Herbert Sutcliffe's 1,481 at 59.24). PA praised Hammond's record performance, saying that his "pulling, cutting and driving can seldom have been equalled". But it added that "the bowling, with the exception of the two Otago men, Badcock and Dunning, was, however, generally mediocre, while the fielding was deplorable". As with Sandham's 325, the prevailing opinion was that Hammond had hammered weak opposition. The London *Star* announced, from a distance of some 11,500 miles: "We must not attempt to rate Hammond's performance in making 336 not out against New Zealand as the equal of Bradman's record score of 334 in England in 1930. England-Australian matches alone are the real tests of great cricketers. Bradman's feat will still be regarded as the greatest until it is surpassed in Tests between England and Australia."

To say that Hammond had a long-standing resentment of Bradman would be akin to saying that Bradman was a fairly good player. No sooner had he established himself as the world's best on the 1928-29 Ashes tour than Hammond was usurped by "the Boy from Bowral". Bradman's success in 1930 demoralised Hammond, who spent much of that summer watching him from first slip. Hammond wasn't even one-third as good as Bradman that year, scoring 306 runs in the five Tests while Bradman hit 26 short of 1,000. Although Hammond tried to seem unflustered by Bradman's statistics, passing them off as mere numbers, those who knew him best detected an attitude bordering on bitterness. Hammond positively envied Bradman – particularly his leg-side play and concentration – and whereas Hammond gave bowlers a smidgen of hope, Bradman killed all hope and danced on its grave. As Neville Cardus wrote: "The difference between Bradman and Hammond can be stated in a few words: Hammond can be kept quiet, Bradman never." Cardus called Hammond "an artist of variable moods", saying that "Hammond in his pomp occasionally suggested that he was batting lazily, without all his mind alert. When at times he scored slowly on a perfect wicket he conveyed to us the impression that he was missing opportunities to get runs because of some absence of mind or indolence of disposition."

Despite Bradman's pre-eminence and unsurpassed standing, many felt Hammond his equal as an off-side player. Bill Bowes wrote that Hammond had "all the mastery and artistry of a Bradman on the off side, but, on the leg side, though his defence was excellent, he was more limited". Len Hutton ventured an alternative view, describing his England team-mate as "the most perfect batsman I ever saw, so much more enjoyable to watch than Sir Don". Hutton said: "To be honest, I preferred to see just an hour of Walter Hammond to eight or ten hours of Don Bradman." Referring to the intense rivalry between them, Hutton added: "I have a feeling somehow that neither Don nor Walter liked each other very much... I'm certain that Walter made 336 against New Zealand in a Test match simply because Don had made 334 against England at Leeds in 1930."

An artist of variable moods: a pensive Hammond in 1936.

For all their rivalry, Hammond and Bradman had much in common – more than they ever cared to admit. Both were introverts who liked their own company, with Hammond a withdrawn, moody figure: in part attributable, thought

David Foot, to the effects of the treatment that he had for his sexual illness as a young man. Bowes called Hammond a "lone wolf" who liked to escape "the atmosphere of cricket". Bob Wyatt remembered "a shy, complex man, one prone to erratic, fickle behaviour". Denis Compton, another England colleague, put it like this: "I was never at ease with him."

The relationship between Hammond and Bradman was always formal, never more than stiffly pleasant. Bradman described him as "a reserved character, inclined to be moody". They parted unhappily in 1946-47 when Hammond led England on his last Ashes tour. Aged 43 and a shadow of his former glory, the increasingly portly, puffed-cheeked Hammond knew that if England were to stand any chance they had to stop Bradman, himself knocking on at 38. In the First Test in Brisbane they thought they'd done it, Bradman seemingly edging a full ball outside his off stump to second slip. The catch to Lancashire batsman Jack Ikin looked so obvious there was no appeal, but Bradman stubbornly stood his ground, claiming it was a bump ball. Hammond, whom one team-mate said was "blazingly angry", was heard to bark: "A fine ******* way to start a series." Bradman had 28 at the time and went on to score 187. Australia won by an innings and took the series 3–0.

By any standards, Hammond's statistics were sensational – one hesitates to say "Bradmanesque". He scored over 50,000 first-class runs, took more than 700 wickets and held over 800 catches. His total of 167 first-class hundreds – including 36 doubles and four triples – has been beaten only by Jack Hobbs (197) and Patsy Hendren (170). However, Hammond played 192 fewer games than Hobbs and 199 fewer than

Hendren, and he topped the English first-class averages for eight straight seasons from 1933.

After retirement, Hammond emigrated to South Africa, home of his second wife. He suffered badly in business and also in a car accident that left him seriously weakened. When he died in 1965, five years after the accident, Hammond left little money for his family having lost his savings in the motoring trade. So acute were his financial problems, a memorial fund was established in England to help his widow and young children. Gloucestershire CCC distributed leaflets seeking donations from its members, the leaflets containing a generous tribute from Bradman, who remarked that he was "very distressed" to hear of the need for the fund. The appeal raised £3,500 (roughly £60,000 today) and was supplemented by the sale of Hammond's trophies and memorabilia.

Hammond and his nemesis Don Bradman – one step ahead in this photograph taken at Trent Bridge in 1938, just as he was throughout their careers.

It was a painful end to a poignant life, one in which Hammond gave so much pleasure yet seemed to derive so little himself. For this most admired and abstruse of men, the New Zealand tour in 1933 brought some of the happiest days that he knew. Hammond loved the far-flung country, the great adventure and sword-fishing trips, and, of course, the warming feeling of having beaten his bête noire Bradman. His pleasure continued on the long voyage home, the players travelling via Fiji, Hawaii, Honolulu and Vancouver before sailing across the Atlantic. When they crossed the International Date Line, meaning that the same day started all over again, Hammond quipped that it would be nice to have that facility in certain games. Relaxed and refreshed, he spent his time playing chess and cards and watching "the passing beauties of the coral reefs and islands". Hammond described England's trip around the world as having "satisfied something deep down inside me", saying: "I had always wanted to go round the globe."

After setting a new record for the highest Test score, he was sitting on top of it, having reached heights not even attained by Bradman.

New Zealand v England

Played at Eden Park, Auckland, on 31 March, 1, 3 April, 1933.
Toss: New Zealand. Result: Match drawn.

NEW ZEALAND

P. E. Whitelaw b Bowes	12	– not out	5
J. E. Mills b Bowes	0	– not out	11
G. L. Weir b Bowes	0		
C. S. Dempster not out	83		
J. L. Kerr lbw b Voce	10		
*M. L. Page st Duckworth b Mitchell	20		
F. T. Badcock b Bowes	1		
†K. C. James b Bowes	0		
J. A. Dunning b Bowes	12		
J. Newman b Voce	5		
D. L. Freeman run out (Paynter/Duckworth)	1		
B 9, lb 4, nb 1	14		

1/0 (2) 2/0 (3) 3/31 (1)   (56.5 overs) 158   (no wkt, 8.3 overs) 16
4/62 (5) 5/98 (6) 6/101 (7)
7/103 (8) 8/123 (9) 9/149 (10) 10/158 (11)

Allen 5–2–11–0; Bowes 19–5–34–6; Mitchell 18–1–49–1; Voce 9.5–3–20–2; Brown 2–0–19–0; Hammond 3–0–11–0. *Second innings* – Allen 3–1–4–0; Bowes 2–0–4–0; Hammond 2–0–6–0; Voce 1.3–0–2–0.

ENGLAND

H. Sutcliffe c Weir b Freeman	24	†G. Duckworth not out	6
*R. E. S. Wyatt b Dunning	60		
W. R. Hammond not out	336	B 7, lb 6, w 1, nb 5	19
E. Paynter b Dunning	36		
L. E. G. Ames b Badcock	26	1/56 (1) (7 wkts dec, 156 overs) 548	
G. O. B. Allen b Badcock	12	2/139 (2) 3/288 (4)	
F. R. Brown c Page b Weir	13	4/347 (5) 5/407 (6)	
W. Voce b Weir	16	6/456 (7) 7/500 (8)	

W. E. Bowes and T. B. Mitchell did not bat.

Badcock 59–16–126–2; Dunning 43–5–156–2; Freeman 20–1–91–1; Newman 17–2–87–0; Page 6–2–30–0; Weir 11–2–39–2.

Umpires: K. H. Cave and J. L. Forrester.

7

Len Hutton (364)
England versus Australia
The Oval 1938

If Don Bradman had a pound for everyone who claimed to have seen his 334 at Headingley in 1930, it would have come to considerably more than the £1,000 gift he received for making the score. Sport is littered with examples of spectators insisting that they saw some famous performance only for their total to exceed the number of seats in the venue. More people supposedly watched the miracle of Headingley '81, for example, when Ian Botham and Bob Willis helped England beat Australia, than could conceivably have filled the same Yorkshire ground; ditto those who claim that they saw Geoffrey Boycott's 100th hundred in the 1977 Headingley Ashes Test. One man who definitely saw Bradman's famous innings, however, was Len Hutton, then a 14-year-old Yorkshire schoolboy who, in the Oval Test of 1938, beat not only Bradman's Ashes record but also Wally Hammond's mark for the highest Test score.

Bradman's 334 had a magical effect on the teenage Hutton. He'd first attended the Yorkshire nets earlier that year and was at an impressionable age. On that summer's day in 1930, Hutton took the penny bus ride from his home in Pudsey, a market town about six miles from Headingley, then a tram to the ground from Stanningley Bottom. He watched spellbound in short trousers from behind the square boundary, munching on sandwiches as Bradman made history. "I was enthralled," he wrote. "No aspiring ballerina at a first sight of Pavlova could have been more uplifted and transported to a land of wonderment than I was on that July day."

At the start of the month, Hutton had gone home dejected after his first sight of Bradman ended in a flash. He was out for one in the Australians' tour match against Yorkshire at Bradford, an isolated failure in a summer of plenty. Now, after watching Bradman beat "Tip" Foster's Ashes record, Hutton dashed home, recruited two willing bowlers and practised "until the night closed around me".

The next time that Hutton saw a Test match was when he was part of its cast list on debut against New Zealand at Lord's in 1937. It was the week of his 21st birthday and he was out for a duck, completing an unwanted hat-trick after he also failed to score on his maiden appearance for the Yorkshire first and second teams. Hutton managed only one run in the second innings of his Test debut too, but he hit an even 100 in the next game in Manchester before another low score in the final fixture at The Oval. Hutton kept his place for England's next Test, the first of his famous 1938 summer, scoring another round 100 against Australia at Trent Bridge, in the process earning a mild rebuke from his Yorkshire team-mate Herbert Sutcliffe as getting out for 100 exactly "looks bad" and you should ideally "add 20 more or so". It was during this innings that Hutton first spoke to Bradman, telling the Australian captain, with a lingering hint of hero worship, that he'd seen the 334. "As far as I recollect," wrote Hutton, "it did not become a dialogue as he did not answer.

Maybe he had heard the same words so often that he was wincing inside."

Or maybe Bradman was simply preoccupied with trying to work out how to separate Hutton and his opening partner Charles Barnett, a hard-hitting 27-year-old from Gloucestershire. They'd put England in control after Hammond won the toss in his first Test as captain. Barnett's 126 in a stand of 219 with Hutton was famous for him coming within two runs of scoring a hundred before lunch on the first day, a feat no Englishman has achieved in Tests. Instead, Barnett had to wait until the first ball after the break to reach three figures. Eddie Paynter (216*) and Denis Compton (102) also made hay before Hammond declared on 658 for eight, then the highest total against Australia.

When the tourists replied, Stan McCabe produced an even more famous innings, one which compelled Bradman to urge his team-mates on to the players' balcony as they would "never see anything like it again". McCabe scored 232 out of 411, Bradman telling him: "If I could play an innings like that, I'd be a proud man, Stan." Bradman scored 144 not out in the second innings to help Australia to a draw. He hit another hundred in the drawn Second Test at Lord's, where Hammond struck 240 and Hutton failed twice with scores of four and five. The Third Test at Old Trafford was washed out, Hutton missing the Fourth at Headingley after breaking his right middle finger while batting for Yorkshire against Middlesex at Lord's (Bill Edrich, the offending bowler on a dangerous pitch, opened at Leeds in Hutton's place). Once again, Bradman scored a hundred – his third in successive innings at Headingley – as Australia won by five wickets to go 1–0 up and retain the Ashes.

Following the 1932-33 Bodyline series, Australia had enjoyed the upper hand in Ashes battles, winning 2–1 in 1934 and 3–2 in 1936-37. Bradman was at the heart of both triumphs. In 1934 he'd achieved his second successive triple at Leeds (his 304 the closest that anyone had come to beating Hammond's record) followed by scores of 244 and 77 in the final Test at The Oval. In 1936-37 he'd produced successive innings of 270, 26, 212 and 169 to turn the series on its head as Australia recovered from 2–0 down – the only instance in Test history of a team winning a series from that position. With almost a month between the Headingley Test of 1938 and the Fifth and final match at the Oval, Hutton's finger had healed sufficiently for him to gain his sixth Test cap. However, he was woefully short of form and practice having scored 125 runs in ten innings in the previous two months.

Hammond won his fourth successive toss to complete the set, there being no toss during the Manchester washout. Now 35, he'd turned amateur the previous year at the behest of a cricketing establishment unwilling to appoint a professional captain – something that did not happen until Hutton was appointed for India's visit in 1952. The Oval toss was a good one to win, groundsman Austin "Bosser" Martin proudly boasting that his pitch was "built to last to Christmas". A vast, corpulent character with a face "as round as a big brown moon", "Bosser" was known for producing "roads" helped by assistants who lugged a four-ton roller lovingly nicknamed "Bosser's Pet". John Woodcock, the former *Times* cricket correspondent who watched this Test as a boy, said that "Bosser" also bound his pitch with liquid manure and "you could almost smell it from Oval station".

The Test was timeless – the previous ones in the series were four-day affairs – as the overall result still hinged on the outcome, even though the Ashes were settled. England, who recalled Hutton in place of Barnett, reacted to conditions by drafting in an extra batsman – Hutton's Yorkshire team-mate Maurice Leyland. Les Ames, the Kent wicketkeeper, had a finger injury so another Yorkshireman was called up – the uncapped Arthur Wood, one week short of his 40th birthday. With no available train to London from Nottingham, where Yorkshire were about to start a Championship match, Wood was forced to take a taxi to be sure of getting to The Oval on time. When the driver asked for the fare, a whopping seven

The England team for the match at the Oval. Standing (l-r): Bill Edrich, Arthur Fagg (twelfth man), Bill Bowes, Len Hutton, Joe Hardstaff junior, Denis Compton, Arthur Wood. Sitting (l-r): Hedley Verity, Ken Farnes, Wally Hammond (captain), Maurice Leyland, Eddie Paynter.

pounds, 15 shillings (around £300 today), Wood, a short and stocky man of unfailing good humour, quipped that he was paying for the ride, not the taxi. Australia also selected an extra batsman, handing a debut to 22-year-old New South Welshman Sid Barnes in place of pace bowler Ernie McCormick, who had a shoulder problem. McCormick had started the tour disastrously; he was no-balled 19 times in his first three overs in the opening match at Worcester, and 35 times in the game overall.

Before an Oval crowd that rose to around 30,000, with people queuing from 3am to pay the three shillings' entry, Hutton and Bill Edrich faced a new-ball attack of Mervyn Waite and Stan McCabe. Waite, a 27-year-old South Australian all-rounder, was making his second and last Test appearance having only debuted the previous match. McCabe, a handy change bowler of brisk medium, was given extra responsibility in McCormick's absence. *Wisden* felt that "the sight of McCabe and Waite beginning Australia's attack in a Test match was almost ludicrous", and neither made much impression. It needed the introduction of star bowler Bill O'Reilly to make the breakthrough after 45 minutes, the tall, aggressive leg-spinner trapping Edrich lbw for 12 with the score on 29. Moments earlier, Hutton had heard the 32-year-old O'Reilly – nicknamed "Tiger" – complain about the pitch to umpire Frank Chester. "Where's the groundsman's hut?" he'd said. "If I had a gun with me, I'd shoot him."

Hammond sent in Leyland at No. 3 – "an astute move", thought Hutton, as O'Reilly was "less effective against left-handers". Hutton said that when the thickset Leyland, 38, emerged "like an old dreadnought steaming to battle", wearing his Yorkshire cap as he always did when playing for England, O'Reilly – recalling previous unproductive meetings with him – erupted: "Good God, it's that Yorkshire bastard again." As they settled into their stand on a day of watery sunshine, Leyland told his partner that he had O'Reilly "taped" and, "what's more, he knows it". However, Hutton called O'Reilly "a supreme bowler if ever there was one", *Wisden* asserting that O'Reilly was "the one formidable bowler" in Australia's ranks and "emphatically one of the greatest bowlers of all time".

In contrast, the rest of the attack was fairly tame, the tourists' strength lying in batting and fielding. As well as finding "almost ludicrous" the sight of a new-ball pairing of Waite and McCabe, *Wisden* described "Chuck" Fleetwood-Smith, a 30-year-old left-arm spinner, as a bowler of "uncertain length and direction" who "certainly fell below expectations". O'Reilly shouldered a heavy load, particularly in the absence of his long-time leg-spinning sidekick Clarrie Grimmett, who'd been controversially left out of the squad. O'Reilly thought that the 46-year-old Grimmett was still the world's best spinner and said that his omission was "a punishing blow to me and to my plans of attack", with the tiny Grimmett's relentless accuracy complementing O'Reilly's attacking style. Rather than pick Grimmett, his South Australia team-mate, Bradman preferred the leg-spinning talents of Frank Ward, who played only in the first Test at Trent Bridge and went wicketless in 30 overs that cost 142. *Wisden* described Ward, 32, who made four Test appearances, as someone "apt to lose accuracy of length". As for the injured McCormick, who'd been advertised as the fastest Australian to visit England, *Wisden* was even more withering, calling him "the most overrated bowler ever to come here" and "the greatest disappointment of the tour" who "accomplished nothing noteworthy".

Batsman error was the likeliest route to wickets at The Oval. When Hutton had 40 and the score was 91, he should have been stumped off Fleetwood-Smith, who lulled him with a sharp-turning chinaman. One report said that the ball "spun a foot" with Hutton "a long way out of his ground, ploughing the off side". It was a rare mistake that presented Ben Barnett, the 30-year-old Victorian wicketkeeper, with a simple chance that should have been taken. Perhaps the finger that Hutton had broken at Lord's had disturbed his rhythm, for although the fracture had healed, the digit remained sore and it started to bother him as he neared his half-century. "It swelled and grew painful," he wrote. However, it was nothing compared to Bradman's face. "He looked at his wits' end," added Hutton, "puzzling out how to separate us two Tykes."

With Leyland offering kindly support, repeating the words "Keep it up, young Leonard", Hutton played in what *Wisden* termed "correct and fluent style". He scored mainly through late cuts and strokes into the covers, seizing a number of off-side singles. For the most part, though, Hutton was cautious, with Australia's fielding – exemplified by Bradman – supporting accurate if mostly unthreatening bowling. Bradman's captaincy was widely esteemed, Neville Cardus writing in the *Manchester Guardian*: "Bradman's fielding and his eager and sensible captaincy throughout a fearful ordeal were beyond praise; he nursed his bowlers, talked to them, put his arm in theirs between overs, and cheered them up; he was not only the team's captain but the father-confessor and philosopher."

Legend has it that Hutton was told by Hammond to "stay there forever", given that it was a timeless Test. But Hutton rubbished the claim that his captain wanted 1,000 runs – a total which groundsman "Bosser" Martin openly admitted he hoped to see. Although Hutton was given no set orders, Hammond did gesture from the players' balcony when Hutton almost threw it away. The captain motioned him to "cool it" when he jumped out at O'Reilly and launched him fractionally over mid-on as he neared his 150. Hutton reached that figure just before stumps, finishing on 160 out of 347 for one. Leyland had 156, their partnership worth 318.

In contrast to Hutton, Leyland prospered through powerful drives and pulls, but he should have been run out for 140. However, Waite, the bowler, in trying to collect a fast return from batsman Jack Badcock, knocked off the bails before gathering the ball. The biggest black mark against Australia came through their bowlers overstepping. "A curiosity of the day's cricket," wrote *Wisden*, "was that four times a no-ball led either to the wicket being hit or the ball being caught."

As the players left the field, many of the Saturday-evening crowd spilled on to it. There were "roars of laughter", said one report, "when a policeman, in preventing the spectators trespassing on the middle, lost his helmet". Afterwards, some England players visited the cinema but Hutton stayed at the team hotel, talking cricket with his friend and team-mate Hedley Verity. He went to bed early and slept for over ten hours. Reaction to England's favourable position was muted in the press, with the placid pitch and thorny issue of timeless Tests dominating debate. *The Times* nailed its colours firmly to the mast. "Any excuse there may be for time-limitless cricket, or any suggestion it should be more common, was exposed for all to see, the affair reduced to a run-making competition and bowlers regarded essentially as a luxury."

Sunday was a rest day and Verity took Hutton to Bognor Regis for a few relaxing hours on the coast. They lunched with one of Verity's friends and played cricket on the beach. Throughout Hutton's innings, Verity made a point of staying with him during the lunch and tea breaks to help maintain his concentration. "His quiet, natural dignity was an immense source of strength to me throughout those long hours," said Hutton.

On a second day tinged with the oncoming autumn, a shower delayed the start by 25 minutes. Hutton and Leyland soon added the six runs they needed to lift their stand to 324, thereby beating England's record stand for any wicket – the 323 of openers Jack Hobbs and Wilfred Rhodes against Australia at Melbourne in 1912. Criticism of the Oval pitch had little effect on the crowd, which numbered around 28,000 on a late August Monday. One report said that "so tightly packed were spectators around the ring that many cases of fainting occurred among women, who were more predominant than usual".

The cricket followed the same steady lines as day one. Hutton and Leyland played carefully and correctly and had taken that stand to 382 – and the score to 411 – when Leyland was out. Hutton drove O'Reilly into the off side where the diminutive batsman Lindsay Hassett fumbled the ball. But as Leyland tried to steal a second, Hassett recovered to fizz a return to the bowler's end, where Bradman – having dashed in from mid-on – took the ball and broke the stumps.

Hutton, left, and Maurice Leyland during their second-wicket stand of 382, then England's highest for any Test wicket.

In what proved to be his last Test innings, Leyland signed off with a career-best 187 from 438 balls with 17 fours.

Hutton then added 135 with captain Hammond, who made 59 before falling lbw to Fleetwood-Smith's googly – the first of three wickets for nine runs as England slipped from 546 for two to 555 for five. Lancashire's Eddie Paynter was lbw for a fourth-ball duck, playing back to O'Reilly, and Middlesex right-hander Denis Compton bowled for a single pushing at Waite. As they'd patiently waited their turn to bat, Compton jokingly bet Paynter £1 that they wouldn't make ten runs between them. The "rot" was stopped by the elegant Nottinghamshire right-hander Joe Hardstaff junior, who helped Hutton lift the score to 634 for five at stumps (Hutton 300, Hardstaff 40).

Hutton had now passed his first-class best of 271 not out for Yorkshire against Derbyshire at Sheffield the previous year. In beating "Tip" Foster's 287, he'd also achieved the highest score by an Englishman in Ashes cricket. It was only then, said Hutton, that "I began to register that the record was in my grasp". But he was talking about Bradman's 334 Ashes record, not Hammond's world-record 336. As with Bradman's innings, when all the focus had been on whether he could beat Foster as opposed to Sandham, now all interest centred on Hutton's pursuit of Bradman's milestone. Hammond's score was as incidental as Sandham's had been, re-emphasising the primacy of Ashes cricket. According to Compton, even Hammond wanted Hutton to raise the bar. Recalling how Hutton looked tired towards the end of his innings, Compton said: "Wally Hammond, Hedley Verity and Bill Bowes pressed him to keep going. In the end they were keener on Len attempting to beat Don's record than he was." Hutton's Yorkshire team-mate Herbert Sutcliffe urged him to go not just for Bradman's Ashes record, but also for Bradman's first-class record. Telegramming from Trent Bridge, where he'd scored a century on day one of the Championship game from which Arthur Wood had been forced to withdraw, Sutcliffe wrote: "Hearty congratulations. No one more delighted than I. Go for Bradman's 452 record. Congratulations also to Maurice."

After play, Hutton was enticed up to the BBC commentary box. It was the first year that the corporation had televised Test cricket and the earliest days of radio commentary, giving players and their feats greater exposure. Hutton told the nation: "I am looking forward to a good night's rest so that tomorrow I may be able to carry on with the good work. But you know it only takes one ball to get the best batsman out."

Hutton returned to the team hotel above Marylebone Station and slumped into a seat in the lounge. Leyland walked up and diagnosed, "You need a drink, something to build you up," and ordered a port and Guinness. "I was then a strict teetotaller," said Hutton, "and I did as he suggested. It was no good. I should have had five or six. I tossed and turned most of the night, haunted by one face. That of Bill O'Reilly." In contrast to getting over ten hours' sleep after day one, Hutton slept "hardly at all". "I could not help picturing the culmination of my innings… I began to believe that I was going to hit over the straight full toss as soon as I got to the crease or put the ball into silly mid-off's hands." Hutton described that night as "an eternity of sleeplessness and introspection". In the morning, his legs ached and he was stiff all over.

As gorgeous sunshine warmed an expectant crowd of some 30,000, Hutton felt anxious when he resumed his innings. "I felt I had gone too far by then to let everyone down." He scored only 21 in the first hour as Australia attacked him with renewed purpose. Hutton's sedate progress throughout this innings – his strike-rate was 42 runs per 100 balls – typecast him as a cautious player. Hutton, however, was the complete batsman, a man for all seasons, pitches and conditions. "In the Hall of Fame he sits at the high table with the elite," wrote *Wisden*, who added that he was "one of the two most accomplished professional batsmen to have played for his country, the other being Sir Jack Hobbs". Bill O'Reilly said that Hutton's footwork was "as light and sure and confident as Bradman's ever was" and called him "the finished player", whose "control of the game is masterful". John Arlott observed that "a stroke by Hutton had an air of inevitability, as if the bat understood the ball". Of Hutton in

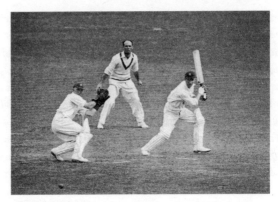

Hutton cuts during the 364.

the midst of gruelling endeavour, Arlott added that "a not unattractive battering of the nose adds a touch of grimness to a face sometimes drawn with exhaustion from the hour-after-hour unwinking concentration of the long innings". Such concentration took its toll on a man of average height, slender build, with keen blue eyes and a pensive exterior.

As Hutton moved closer to Bradman's score, so Bradman moved closer to him. He stationed himself at silly mid-on, breathing down his challenger's neck. "I looked at him and he looked at me," wrote Hutton. "A psychological duel which I had to win." There were gasps when he survived two confident lbw appeals from Fleetwood-Smith. "Unnerving moments," he admitted. Then, at 12.45pm on Tuesday, August 23, 1938, with his score standing at 332, history was made. On the radio, the BBC's Howard Marshall described it:

> *"Here's Fleetwood-Smith again to Hutton. Hutton hits him – oh, beautiful shot. That's the record (cheers). Well, that was the most lovely stroke. A late cut off Fleetwood-Smith's leg-break, which absolutely flashed to the*

boundary for four runs to give Hutton the record,
beating Bradman's record made at Leeds in 1930 of 334.
Beating that record for the highest score ever made by an
individual in Test matches in this country… not just in
this country, but between England and Australia ever
and equalling Hammond's record in Test matches of any
kind made at Auckland in 1933. They're singing…
Terrific reception. The whole crowd is standing up and
cheering. Thousands of them, all round the ground.
They're all standing up. Bradman's been and rushed
across to shake Hutton by the hand. The whole
Australian team have congratulated him. And now
everybody cheering… Oh, it really is a wonderful scene.
Here in this brilliant sunshine, they won't stop cheering."

Bradman was first to congratulate Hutton. He walked up and warmly shook his hand, twice patting him on the back before continuing to applaud as he respectfully retreated. At the bowler's end, Fleetwood-Smith stood, cross-legged, applauding also before coming down the pitch to pay homage. Hardstaff, the non-striker, congratulated Hutton followed by the rest of the Australian side. All, that is, apart from O'Reilly, whom Neville Cardus said was so tired that he "lay prone on the grass until he saw a man coming out with drinks, when he got up at once and made for him in a hurry".

Cardus captured the emotional outpouring, with play held up for several minutes. "The scene which now occurred moved even the hardened critics," he wrote. "Thousands of happy people stood up and cheered. Somebody with a cornet began to play 'For he's a jolly good fellow' and the crowd took up the refrain in that evangelical tone which the British public invariably adopts when it lifts up its heart to rejoice in song. Moreover, the voices and the cornet did not keep

Hutton is congratulated by Don Bradman, whose record he beat, and whose innings he saw as a 14-year-old schoolboy. Also pictured are, from left, "Chuck" Fleetwood-Smith, the bowler, wicketkeeper Ben Barnett and non-striker Joe Hardstaff junior.

together – but in the circumstances I admit that to say so is a piece of pedantic musical criticism."

It was the crowd singing "For he's a jolly good fellow" that moved Hutton's mother to tears as she listened at home while doing the washing. His father had been building a new telephone exchange near Bradford but, every now and again, a boy with a wireless had run across to tell him the score. So lost in the moment was Cardus that he added: "As the ground became resonant with the cheering the thought occurred to me that it was being heard far and wide, all over the Empire, not only all over the country. People walking down Collins Street in Melbourne would hear it, and it would roar and echo in Kandy, Calcutta, Allahabad, Penang: they would hear it in the Cocos Islands and join in, and on liners going patiently their ways over the seven seas they would hear it too, and drink Hutton's health."

They certainly heard it at Trent Bridge, where Yorkshire's Championship match was drifting to a draw. Spectators listening to the radio in the car park sounded their klaxon horns and the players shared the joy when the news became known. "It was some minutes before the game resumed on sober lines," reported the *Nottingham Evening News*. At The Oval, more cheers followed when Hutton passed Hammond's 336, but they were not nearly so loud or widespread. Once again, Bradman's record was the one that counted, with Hammond's regarded as secondary detail.

At lunch, Hutton had 361 and eclipsed the ground record of 357 not out by Surrey's Bobby Abel against Somerset in 1899. With the total now 758 for five, Cardus quipped: "I observed now a number of Chelsea veterans watching the cricket. I wondered how many of them would live to see the match finished." Hutton added three more runs after the interval before lofting O'Reilly to Hassett at cover. He'd batted for 13 hours, 17 minutes and faced 847 balls, his 364 including 35 fours, 15 threes, 18 twos and 143 singles. Hutton's was the longest first-class innings at the time but is not even in the top ten now. When he passed Bradman's mark, he'd been batting for 12 hours, 19 minutes as opposed to Bradman's six hours, 23 minutes.

Hutton's departure left England 770 for six but still there was no declaration from Hammond, or need for one in a timeless match. Wood injected a brisk 53, joking that he was always "a man for a crisis". After his dismissal left the score 876 for seven, Wood – with deadpan demeanour – told "Bosser" Martin that he'd seen some holes in the pitch. "Holes?" shot back "Bosser", horrified. "Aye," replied Wood.

"Six where t'stumps go in." When the total was 887 for seven, equalling the first-class record in England, Australia's problems became even worse. Bradman, bowling his occasional leg-spin at the Vauxhall End, slipped in one of the footholes left by O'Reilly and "fell to the ground in utter collapse". The crowd stood silent as the maestro was shouldered from the field like a wounded soldier lifted from the trenches. O'Reilly, who never liked Bradman, found the situation preposterous. "You'd swear I was an opal miner," he said, referencing the supposed depth of the footholes. "The crowd that came out to cart him off, you'd swear it was an aeroplane disaster. We didn't see him again on the tour. We waved him goodbye as he left the field, never laid eyes on him again until we got on the ship to go home." Bradman was diagnosed with a fractured right ankle and with opening batsman Jack Fingleton having earlier torn a leg muscle, Australia were effectively down to nine men. Only now did Hammond declare at tea on day three, safe in the knowledge that Bradman – the one man who could conceivably have helped Australia to a comparable score – couldn't bat. Otherwise, he might have let the innings run its course.

England's 903 for seven, with Hardstaff undefeated on 169, beat the previous highest Test total of 849 when Sandham hit his 325. It is still the highest total achieved in England and remained the Test record until 1997, when Sri Lanka scored 952 for six declared against India in Colombo. Fleetwood-Smith bowled 87 of the 335.2 overs delivered by Australia at The Oval, his figures of one for 298 the most expensive in Tests. "You woke up in the night time and your arm was still going around," he groaned. O'Reilly, who bowled only two fewer overs for the comparatively frugal return of three for 178, wore the skin off a finger. Without Bradman ("like watching *Hamlet* without the Prince", thought the

Telegraph), Australia folded. They were bowled out for 201 and 123, England winning by a record margin of an innings and 579 runs before tea on day four. Such was Yorkshire's contribution to the triumph that its five representatives scored 612 of the 903 runs, took ten of the 16 wickets and held four catches. In recognition, the crowd struck up a rendition of *On Ilkla Moor Baht'at* in front of the pavilion.

More than 500 congratulatory messages were sent to Hutton at the ground. One of the first came from the seaside village of Aberdovey, Gwynedd, on the west coast of Wales from "Tip" Foster's 89-year-old mother: "Cordial congratulations from the mother of R. E. Foster and all Aberdovey sportsmen," a gesture that touched him deeply. Back home in Pudsey, the parish church bells rang a peal of 364 chimes, the bells sounding for half an hour pulled by eight ringers. The following Sunday, hymn No. 364 was the most popular in several Yorkshire churches, the first two lines adapted by some of the more whimsical worshippers to read: "All hail the power of Hutton's name. Let Aussies prostrate fall." Arthur Whitelaw, the Australian businessman who'd given Bradman his £1,000 gift at Headingley in 1930, extended the same generosity to Hutton. "Len was always a thrifty lad," his father told the papers. "He'll not waste it." Hutton bought his first car with the money – a bullet nose Morris for £125 (about £5,000 now). Perhaps the one disappointment – as a housewife had rushed to tell him on leaving The Oval – was that he hadn't scored one more run, "and then you'd have had a run for every day of the year".

Although Hutton's innings was widely praised, the pitch was castigated in the press. Cardus lambasted a surface "not in the interests of cricket" and said that the game left "an unpleasant taste". He added that "no cricket match should occur again in which the wicket is contrived so that an innings of 900 is possible against any bowling". The *Telegraph* said the wicket "completely destroyed the balance of the game", insisting: "It is surely high time the authorities stepped in and made an end of such harmful nonsense." In the following year's *Wisden*, Bradman wrote a powerful piece entitled "Cricket at the Crossroads". He feared that the game was becoming less attractive to spectators. Bradman said he was "satisfied that some groundsmen can, and do, dope their wickets", adding that the effect was to produce a pitch "useless to any type of bowler".

After his record-breaking innings, Hutton was acclaimed England's answer to Bradman. The comparison troubled him for he did not consider himself nearly as good. Hutton came to view the 364 as an albatross and said that the thought

"Bosser" Martin, the Oval groundsman, pictured with his giant roller in front of a scoreboard showing England's equally giant total.

of people going specifically to watch him bat, of fathers taking their excited sons to see him play, "bothered me no end". His privacy shrank and he came to understand the burden that Bradman carried. Hutton wondered whether the innings "was not the second-worst happening of my career", the worst being an injury to his left arm suffered during wartime commando training that left it two inches shorter than his right. "I was famous overnight, and I wondered what had hit me," he said. "The first thing I remember was getting a call from Billy Butlin asking me to go down to Skegness and judge a bathing-beauty contest. They offered to send a Rolls-Royce for me."

Hutton was naturally shy and retiring. His first meeting with the great Jack Hobbs had left him tongue-tied – "I gaped and no words came". He felt like a "youthful interloper" when he first entered the Yorkshire dressing-room, which he reverentially termed "the holy of holies". Hutton came from an unusual background – the Moravian community in Fulneck, Pudsey. The Moravians were the earliest Protestant sect in 15th-century Europe (Hutton's mother was a descendant) and they preached the virtues of hard work and discipline. J. M. Kilburn described Hutton as "a man whom it would be difficult greatly to like or dislike", someone who inspired neutral feelings. There was something in Hutton of Bradman perhaps, for he, too, gave little away.

The Ashes stayed with Australia until 1953 when Hutton led England to a 1–0 win in Coronation year. He retained them in 1954-55 – England's first series triumph Down Under since Bodyline. Hutton lost six years to the Second World War – he was 23 when it broke out – but still scored more than 40,000 first-class runs at an average over 55, with 129 hundreds.

He was knighted in 1956, served as an England selector and also as Yorkshire CCC president. In later life, Hutton lived in Kingston, Surrey, where he died in September 1990, aged 74.

Hutton's 364 is still celebrated each year at Headingley. In 2003, Keith Moss, the then Yorkshire chairman, founded the Sir Leonard Hutton 364 Club, which holds an annual dinner at the ground. Moss, whose grandparents were neighbours of the Huttons at Fulneck, has attracted many notable speakers including Sir Garry Sobers and Sir John Major. Around 350 guests talk cricket and celebrate Hutton's innings, life and career. In 1988, the 50th anniversary of the record score, Moss co-organised a gala dinner in Leeds to mark it. Hutton was guest of honour and many of his English and Australian peers were present, including Ray Lindwall and Keith Miller, who flew in from Australia. Hutton signed many menus and his eyes twinkled at television footage of the innings. Among the tributes was one sent by Bradman:

> *"Advancing years do not cloud my memory of Len's mammoth innings, described in Wisden as 'the most remarkable exhibition of concentration and endurance ever seen on the cricket field'. So, on the fiftieth anniversary of this fact, I salute once more this milestone which has remained an achievement dear to the hearts of all Yorkshiremen. The passage of time has taken from our midst many of Len's pals and mine from the two teams, but happily Len is still with us dispensing appropriate words of wisdom. I salute him as one of the great craftsmen of all time, whose skill and style was the envy of us all. Congratulations, Len, on the fiftieth anniversary of your never-to-be-forgotten performance, and I'm proud to remember that I was the first to shake you by the hand."*

England v Australia

Played at Kennington Oval, London, on 20, 22, 23, 24 August, 1938.

Toss: England. Result: England won by an innings and 579 runs.

ENGLAND

L. Hutton c Hassett b O'Reilly	364	†A. Wood c and b Barnes	53
W. J. Edrich lbw b O'Reilly	12	H. Verity not out	8
M. Leyland run out (Hassett/Bradman)	187	B 22, lb 19, w 1, nb 8	50
*W. R. Hammond lbw b Fleetwood-Smith	59		
E. Paynter lbw b O'Reilly	0	1/29 (2) (7 wkts dec, 335.2 overs) 903	
D. C. S. Compton b Waite	1	2/411 (3) 3/546 (4)	
J. Hardstaff jnr not out	169	4/547 (5) 5/555 (6) 6/770 (1) 7/876 (8)	

K. Farnes and W. E. Bowes did not bat.

Waite 72–16–150–1; McCabe 38–8–85–0; O'Reilly 85–26–178–3; Fleetwood-Smith
87–11–298–1; Barnes 38–3–84–1; Hassett 13–2–52–0; Bradman 2.2–1–6–0.

AUSTRALIA

W. A. Brown c Hammond b Leyland	69	– c Edrich b Farnes	15
C. L. Badcock c Hardstaff b Bowes	0	– b Bowes	9
S. J. McCabe c Edrich b Farnes	14	– c Wood b Farnes	2
A. L. Hassett c Compton b Edrich	42	– lbw b Bowes	10
S. G. Barnes b Bowes	41	– lbw b Verity	33
†B. A. Barnett c Wood b Bowes	2	– b Farnes	46
M. G. Waite b Bowes	8	– c Edrich b Verity	0
W. J. O'Reilly c Wood b Bowes	0	– not out	7
L. O. Fleetwood-Smith not out	16	– c Leyland b Farnes	0
*D. G. Bradman absent hurt	–	absent hurt	
J. H. W. Fingleton absent hurt	–	absent hurt	
B 4, lb 2, nb 3	9	B 1	1

1/0 (2) 2/19 (3)	(52.1 overs) 201	1/15 (2) 2/18 (3) (34.1 overs) 123	
3/70 (4) 4/145 (5) 5/147 (6)		3/35 (4) 4/41 (1) 5/115 (5)	
6/160 (7) 7/160 (8) 8/201 (1)		6/115 (7) 7/117 (6) 8/123 (9)	

Farnes 13–2–54–1; Bowes 19–3–49–5; Edrich 10–2–55–1; Verity 5–1–15–0;
Leyland 3.1–0–11–1; Hammond 2–0–8–0. *Second innings*—Farnes 12.1–1–63–4;
Bowes 10–3–25–2; Leyland 5–0–19–0; Verity 7–3–15–2.

Umpires: F. Chester and F. I. Walden.

8

Garry Sobers (365*)
West Indies versus Pakistan
Jamaica 1958

If Len Hutton's 364 against Australia at The Oval in 1938 was his most famous innings, his finest hour was arguably when he scored 205 against the West Indies in Jamaica in 1954. It was the last of his 19 Test hundreds, the first double-century by an England captain in an overseas Test, and it led his side to a victory that saw them draw the series from 2–0 down. In suffocating heat, after England had bowled out the West Indies for 139, Hutton made his runs out of 414 and had been on the field for nearly three days when he was out. "It was an infinitely greater endurance performance than that at The Oval in 1938," wrote his biographer, Gerald Howat. *Wisden* said that "for concentration and control, Hutton's innings of a shade under nine hours scarcely could have been excelled". It was during this match – at the end of a series that *The Times* described as "the second most controversial" after Bodyline, blighted as it was by political infighting and off-field controversy – that West Indies handed a debut to what *Wisden* also described as "a 17-year-old left-arm slow bowler and useful batsman, who showed distinct promise". The teenager returned his team's best figures of four for 75 in England's first innings and, batting at No. 9, made scores of 14 not out and 26. Hutton was impressed, recalling that the youngster batted with "such skill and aplomb that a rapid rise in the order was fully forecast". He added: "Little did I imagine that I was playing against a batsman who was eventually to break my record Test score... Garfield St Aubrun Sobers had arrived."

An injury to Alf Valentine, West Indies' first-choice left-arm spinner, had paved the way for Sobers's debut. When he got word of his call-up, he was playing cricket with his brothers and friends at home in Barbados. "My heart beat faster and all sorts of things flashed through my mind," he said. "Here I was, a teenager in short pants, being told I was wanted by the West Indies to play along with the Three Ws, Walcott, Weekes and Worrell." Four years later, when he captured the record, Sobers was classed as a genuine all-rounder. The rapid rise in the order that many had forecast had seen him fill several batting positions. He'd even opened before settling at No. 3 for the visit of Pakistan in 1957-58, the first meeting between the nations after Pakistan entered Test cricket in 1952. After scoring 52 in the drawn First Test in Barbados, though, and 52 and 80 in the hosts' 120-run victory in the Second in Trinidad, still one thing eluded Sobers going into the third of the five-match series in Jamaica – a Test hundred.

Pursuit of a maiden three-figure score had dogged him since facing Hutton's men. This was his 17th Test and, in 28 innings, he'd scored 856 runs at an average of 34.24, with his 80 against Pakistan in Trinidad his highest score. Sobers had made two first-class hundreds for his native Barbados, including an unbeaten 183 against the Pakistanis only the previous month, plus three on the 1957 tour of England, including a career-best 219 not out against Nottinghamshire, his future county. But amid whispers that he wasn't quite cutting it so high in the order, there was pressure on him at Sabina Park. "I don't mind admitting that I was becoming a little anxious about it," he wrote. "I was really determined to make the breakthrough. I had scored centuries in inter-island cricket in the West Indies and on tour. So why not in the Tests?" But whereas his critics were sharpening their knives, Sobers felt confident deep down. The maiden Test century that followed was not just a record-breaking triple but also the first of six Test hundreds in the space of ten innings, the floodgates positively bursting apart.

Sobers certainly had no better chance to shake off the monkey than during the spring of 1958. Against what he openly admitted was "hardly a devilish attack", and on a fast and bouncy Jamaica pitch – exactly the sort that he liked as he preferred the ball coming on to the bat – he thought: 'It's now or never.' After Pakistan chose to bat and scored 328, opener Imtiaz Ahmed striking 122, Sobers's quest was given a major boost when Pakistan lost two bowlers – half their attack – before he'd properly got his eye in. Mahmood Hussain, a 25-year-old considered their fastest bowler, broke down after just five balls of the innings. Opener Conrad Hunte pushed a ball back down the pitch and Mahmood tore a groin as he tried to stop it. Then, after bowling just 15 overs, left-arm spinner Nasim-ul-Ghani – then the youngest Test player at 16 – broke his right thumb when fielding a ball. Neither took further part, Pakistan thus reduced to nine batsmen as Australia had been at The Oval in 1938 following the injuries to Jack Fingleton and Don Bradman.

The loss of Mahmood and Nasim put a huge strain on the two remaining frontline bowlers: pacemen Fazal Mahmood and Khan Mohammad. Fazal, 31, the first great bowler of Pakistan cricket, would send down 85.2 overs from his tall, flowing action, the most by a pace bowler in a Test innings. Khan, a strapping 30-year-old, would deliver 54 overs and both would concede over 200 runs. In addition, Abdul Kardar, the captain and father of Pakistan cricket, who'd led them in their inaugural Test against India in 1952, would feel compelled to bowl despite starting the match with a broken finger on his left hand. Kardar, a 33-year-old who'd played for India on their 1946 tour to England as "Abdul Hafeez", would supply 37 overs of left-arm spin against doctor's orders; he'd been told to stop bowling for at least three weeks. Pakistan would use nine bowlers in total, with only wicketkeeper Imtiaz and batsman Wazir Mohammad not called on.

With the tourists so badly depleted, Sobers said "this was one opportunity I wasn't going to let go". He'd come to the crease at 4.20pm just after tea on day two and received, in the words of local newspaper the *Daily Gleaner*, "a deafening ovation such as an ingoing batsman who has hit a century is given". A crowd of around 10,000 watched in glorious weather, many spectators wearing light-green cardboard sunshades which had been freely distributed by a local firm. The score was 87 for one, Rohan Kanhai, a 22-year-old future West Indies captain, having just been caught behind off Fazal after batting, felt the *Gleaner*, "like a prisoner in chains" for 25 runs in almost two hours. Sobers, whose modus operandi usually varied between attack and all-out attack, was soon cover-driving and pulling to the boundary, ending the day on 20. Just before stumps, Hunte, a trim and athletic 25-year-old, reached his second hundred in three Tests having struck 142 on debut in the first Test in Barbados.

West Indies closed on 147 for one, 181 behind, already promisingly placed on a docile pitch.

Since drawing 1–1 with England in 1929-30, when Andy Sandham had taken the record, West Indies had made promising progress generally in Test cricket. They'd beaten England 2–1 at home in 1934-35, their maiden Test-series triumph, and achieved a 2–0 victory on England's next visit in 1947-48. In 1950, they'd gained their first series win on English soil, a shock 3–1 success thanks, in no small part, to "those two little pals of mine, Ramadhin and Valentine" – Sonny Ramadhin and Alf Valentine spinning their way to 59 wickets in the four Tests. Although West Indies had struggled in their meetings with Australia, and also lost 3–0 on their 1957 trip to England, a powerful team was starting to emerge, with Sobers at its beating heart. Pakistan, meanwhile, had lost only one of their five Test series – their inaugural one in 1952-53, when they'd gone down 2–1 in India. They'd followed that with a 1–1 draw in England in 1954 and a 0–0 draw when India visited the following winter, when all five Tests ended in stalemate. Two–nil and 1–0 triumphs at home to New Zealand and Australia respectively had sent them into the 1957-58 Caribbean series in fine fettle. Under Kardar's inspired leadership, *Wisden* said that Test cricket's newcomers "at once made themselves worthy of respect rather than anyone's sympathy".

The strength of West Indies and Pakistan lay in their batting, as the Jamaica Test would emphasise again. The tone for a high-scoring series had been set in the First Test when Hanif Mohammad, a pint-sized 23-year-old opener, almost beat Hutton's record himself. After West Indies scored 579 for

"The Little Master" – Pakistan opener Hanif Mohammad.

nine declared, Everton Weekes striking 197 to go with Hunte's debut hundred, Pakistan made 106 and were forced to follow on, 473 behind. Around three and a half days were left (all five Tests were six-day affairs) and even Hanif thought they were doomed. "Everyone was feeling it was a formality to get Pakistan out," he wrote. "I must confess that we too did not feel that we could last for three and a half days to survive defeat." But against an attack led by Roy Gilchrist, a 23-year-old of terrifying pace and comparable temperament, Hanif produced one of cricket's most famous defensive innings, scoring 337 in 16 hours, ten minutes (Hanif claimed that he batted for 16 hours, 39 minutes in what, at any rate, was the longest first-class innings at the time and second-highest Test score). Bruised and battered by Gilchrist's speed, which he admitted "totally shattered my confidence", Hanif somehow survived until just after tea on day six, by which time the game was safe. He fell to a catch by wicketkeeper Gerry Alexander in trying to steer a ball from medium-pacer Denis Atkinson past the slips, 28 short of taking the record. A year later, Hanif, a classical right-hander known as "The Little Master", long before the sobriquet fell on Sachin Tendulkar, beat Bradman's first-class record of 452 not out. Hanif scored 499 for Karachi against Bahawalpur in Karachi, running himself out in pursuit of a quintuple-century.

For Sobers, a mere hundred, let alone a quintuple, would have been more than enough at Sabina Park. Conditions were perfect as he resumed on day three, the sun gleaming off the wooden stands that held around 15,000 spectators. Sobers stroked three fours in quick succession off Khan Mohammad: a delicate leg glance, a cheeky dab just wide of the slips and a thumping square drive as he reached his fourth consecutive fifty of the series. Hunte scored heavily on the leg side especially, the pair highlighting the paucity of Pakistan's total.

They made for something of an heroic duo, with both having risen from humble circumstances in Barbados: Hunte as one of nine children whose father worked on a sugar plantation, Sobers as one of seven whose merchant-seaman father drowned when his ship was torpedoed by a U-boat in the Atlantic when Sobers was five. Hunte was a naturally aggressive player, although he later subdued those instincts to become a selfless rock at the top of the order at a time when West Indies had too many stylists and not enough rocks. Hunte left cricket in his mid-thirties to commit his life to Moral Re-Armament, an international moral/spiritual movement. In later years he helped to develop cricketing talent in black townships as South African apartheid crumbled.

At lunch, Hunte had 139, Sobers 76, and the total was 243 for one. Sobers breezed past his previous best of 80 in the preceding Test and powered confidently through the nineties, the crowd willing him on in his century quest. At last, the longed-for moment finally came, Sobers pushing a ball from Kardar to square leg, contemplating a quick single and then changing his mind, only for the return from Saeed Ahmed to be so wild that he was able to scamper an overthrow. "The ovation that Sobers received from this crowd was positively amazing," said the *Gleaner*. "It could not have been beaten anywhere in the world." Perhaps momentarily disturbed by the joy of the moment, Sobers edged a ball from Kardar just short of slip, the closest to a chance that he gave in his innings. Normal service was soon resumed, Sobers slashing Fazal to the square-leg boundary to raise West Indies' 300, then pulling, square-cutting and cover-driving Khan for boundaries in the space of an over, racing along to his 150.

At tea, Sobers had 170 and the score was 400 for one. Hunte – 196 at the break – reached 200 and, when Sobers followed him to the mark, it was only the second time that two batsmen had scored double-hundreds in the same Test innings (Don Bradman and Sid Barnes having done so for Australia against England at Sydney in 1946). Once again, Sobers got there in the act of overthrows, pushing Khan into the off side and calling Hunte through for a single. Hanif swooped at cover and threw down the stumps, the ball flying to the boundary to take Sobers from 199 to 204. At stumps, the second-wicket pair were still together, having batted through day three to lift their team to 504 for one. Sobers's share was 228, a new first-class best, as was Hunte's 242. Despite a scoreboard that made horrific reading for them, the tourists were praised. "Pakistan must be admired for the plucky manner in which they stuck to their task," averred the *Gleaner*. "Less courageous mortals would have sent up the distress signal. With the odds stacked against them, they smiled and carried on. Congratulations to them." Principal talk was not of Pakistan, however, but of records, with both Sobers and Hunte having the chance to go past Hutton. Time was no issue with three days left, and with West Indies keen to bat Pakistan out of the match.

That night, as the historic possibilities raced around his head, Sobers tossed and turned as Hutton had done 20 years earlier. "Normally I sleep well when I eventually go to bed," he wrote, "admittedly later than most people, but on this occasion I had a restless night. Perhaps because of the talk of records and the possibilities the next day, I found myself lying awake. This was before the days when the team doctor gave players sleeping tablets." It wasn't just the highest individual score in Test cricket that beckoned the batsmen on day four, but also the highest Test partnership – then 451 by Bill Ponsford and Don Bradman for the second wicket against England at The Oval in 1934. The two West Indians had shared 417 when they resumed on another glorious morning, and they'd taken that to 446 when Hunte was calamitously run out. Seeking a single which he wrongly thought would break the record, Hunte pushed Khan to substitute fielder Ijaz Butt at midwicket and was comfortably beaten by his throw to the bowler's end. Sobers described Hunte's departure for 260 as a "tragedy" and a "waste" as he

Garry Sobers, right, and Conrad Hunte resume their epic second-wicket stand of 446.

was "seeing the ball as big as a breadfruit". He added: "I was seeing the ball like a breadfruit, too, and I didn't intend throwing my hand away."

Within minutes, though, he very nearly did. On 248, Sobers dashed up the pitch when Everton Weekes, the new batsman, pushed Khan to midwicket. To Sobers's horror, Weekes stood motionless, as if frozen to the spot, as both players finished up at the same end. But instead of throwing to the bowler's end, Waqar Hasan, another substitute, threw the ball to the wicketkeeper, giving Sobers time to regain his ground. "That was the only time I could have been out in my innings," he said. Sobers celebrated the escape by cover-driving Khan to reach his 250 and, at lunch, he had 265 out of 592 for two. As excitement built at the prospect of Hutton's record falling, the gates were closed during the interval, the crowd having risen to a ground-bursting 25,000.

Weekes added six to his lunchtime score then was caught at slip for 39. It was a slower ball from Fazal and Weekes flashed hard at it, Hanif holding a brilliant low chance. Sobers now had 269 and two more took him past the highest Test score by a West Indian – George Headley's 270 not out against England at the same ground in 1935. "The crowd gave him an ovation which must have been heard back in Barbados," said the *Gleaner*.

Sobers had now been joined by Clyde Walcott, the junior member of the Three Ws, the famous batting trio born within 18 months of each other in Barbados. Frank Worrell, the oldest and most stylish of the three, did not play in this series as he was studying for an economics degree at Manchester University (Worrell had close links with the area having played for Radcliffe in the Lancashire League). In 1960 Worrell made history by becoming West Indies' first full-time black captain; in 1958, however, the West Indian captain was still a white man – in this case, Gerry Alexander, a Cambridge-educated wicketkeeper who'd made only two Test appearances. At a time when West Indies had yet to gain independence from colonial rule, Alexander was chosen ahead of superior candidates such as Walcott and Weekes, both of whom announced their retirement from Test cricket during this series in their early thirties (Walcott, however, returned for two matches against England in 1960).

The savage strokeplay of Walcott, vividly described by the cricket writer David Frith as "an unforgettable mix of silk and gently rolling thunder", was gloriously evidenced by one shot especially at Sabina Park. "Walcott electrified the crowd by hitting Kardar for one of the biggest sixes seen on this ground, as the ball went soaring over the north-western bleachers into Melbourne Road," said the *Gleaner*. "Play was held up for five minutes until the ball was found." The crowd was on its feet again when Sobers went to his triple-century in ten minutes short of nine hours with a single off Fazal. "By that time the place was humming," he said. "Sabina Park is a small ground and, in those days, with spectators hanging on to the light pylons, dangling from trees and with their legs through the double-decked stands at the northern end, it was like a bull-ring. It was then, and only then, that I settled in my mind that I could get that Hutton record – in fact, that I *would* get that record."

Although hardly a novice in his 17th Test, Sobers was still a wide-eyed youngster of 21, unaccustomed to what was now unfolding. Walcott, 32, was a fount of wisdom, guiding him on like an older brother. "Clyde kept urging me on: 'Settle down, take it easy. The runs will come and I'll give you as much of the strike as possible.'" Sobers added: "The way I approached it was to tell myself that I had just come in to bat, that I didn't have 300 on the board and that, instead, I only needed to score 65 to win the match or to post 1,000 for the season." Despite his sleepless night, Sobers did not feel tired as adrenaline kicked in. "I felt good. The noise from the spectators, many in trees and on pylons, was incredible." A late cut for two off Fazal took Sobers past Sandham's 325 at the venue where he'd made it 28 years earlier. At tea, he had 336 – having beaten Don Bradman and equalled Wally Hammond – out of 760 for three, a lead, if anyone cared at this point, of 432. A brace of singles off Fazal then took Sobers past Hanif's 337 earlier in the series,

Hanif dashing in from cover to shake his hand in echoes of Bradman's acknowledgement of Hutton at The Oval. The highest first-class score in the West Indies, George Headley's 344 not out for Jamaica against Lord Tennyson's XI in 1932, was next to fall, an achievement that drew a smattering of applause.

Loud cheers greeted Sobers's seventh half-century, made in the nerveless time of 66 minutes. When Sobers had 363, just two short of glory, Kardar sportingly brought on Hanif to bowl his very occasional, harmless off-spin. Even more sportingly, Hanif asked if he could bowl left-handed, to which Sobers quipped: "You can bowl with both hands if you like." With Hanif now bowling with his wrong hand, Sobers pushed a single to long-off to tie the record. Then, from the first legitimate ball of the next over (the first being a wide), Fazal rapped him on the pads and roared an appeal as Kingston held its breath. "Not out," said umpire Tom Ewart. Sobers nudged Fazal's next ball into the covers, Walcott called him through for a single and the world record fell amid riotous scenes. "In a split second, the place was pure bedlam," wrote Sobers. "The crowd streamed across the ground and lifted me in the air and, for a time, I was on cloud nine – almost literally. It is impossible for me to adequately describe my feelings at that moment."

Such was the surge to congratulate Sobers, the pitch was damaged by the onrushing crowd, causing play to be abandoned for the day even though an hour remained. Pakistan, not so sporting that they didn't sense a perfect opportunity to take time out of the game, complained about a particular spot at the southern end, the clock ticking down while it was repaired. Amid the hive of groundstaff activity, West Indies declared on 790 for three (Walcott 88), eclipsing their previous highest Test total of 681 for six against England at Trinidad in 1954. Sobers's 365 had spanned ten hours, 14 minutes – three hours, three minutes faster than Hutton – and comprised one five, 38 fours, six threes, 30 twos and 130 singles.

L. D. Roberts, the *Gleaner* sports editor, lambasted the crowd's behaviour, which he felt denied West Indies late wickets against tired and dispirited opponents and/or Sobers the chance to reach 400. "I attach blame all round for what happened after Sobers made Test history," he announced. "It was an achievement for all West Indians to crow about and for those of us who choose to get drunk about it to do so. But at the right time and in the proper place. There can be no excuse for that show of bad manners, for that was all that it was when the events are viewed in their proper perspective. Those in charge of arrangements for the match should have had the foresight to guard against the likelihood of such a thing happening and had a significant number of policemen on hand." Roberts said that wicketkeeper Imtiaz was "almost too tired to throw the ball back to the bowler" after more than two days in the field, "while Hanif, Saeed and company were all very tired little men".

A rest day followed, and Pakistan found energy from somewhere on day five to reach a respectable 273 for five after starting their second innings 452 behind. Before a 15,000 crowd, swelled by hundreds of children as schools had closed to allow them to go, Wazir Mohammad scored an unbeaten 102 and captain Kardar an undefeated 46. However, it was a task too far to repeat their Hanif-inspired survival in Barbados, particularly with only three wickets needed on the final day as the tourists were missing their two injured bowlers. They added only 15 more runs before sinking to defeat by an innings and 174, West Indies taking a 2–0 lead with two Tests to play.

Afterwards, Kardar praised Sobers's record innings. "I have seen all the great left-handers and Sobers surpassed them all," he said. "He is a very great player, and I am glad I had the pleasure of seeing this innings of his. I hope he will go on for a long time to be of help to the West Indies." Jeff Stollmeyer, Sobers's first Test captain, said that the 365 was "the more remarkable when it is considered that the lad is only 21". Hutton cabled his congratulations and, in a newspaper interview, described it as "a magnificent effort", saying that he thought Sobers would only improve. He added that he was not surprised that the record had fallen in this series as "it seemed that the conditions were ripe for record-breaking". However, he was surprised that Sobers was the man to do it, thinking that he might be too impetuous to play such an innings. In recognition of it, Sobers received the key to the city of Kingston and, when he returned home to Barbados, a motorcade through the crowded streets. "It was as joyous an occasion for them as it was for me to think that their own 21-year-old should have broken this record," he said.

With his hundred hoodoo finally over, Sobers hit two more in an eight-wicket victory in the Fourth Test in Georgetown (125 and 109 not out). In transit to the game, his new-found celebrity was clear when he landed in Trinidad, one report stating: "A large crowd at Piarco airport last night greeted Garfield Sobers like a film star. There were cheers as the young West Indian batsman walked from the plane to the terminal building. Then he was besieged by autograph hunters." Sobers came down from cloud nine in the final Test in Trinidad, making 14 and 27 as Pakistan won by an innings and one run to make the final result 3–1 to the West Indies. Sobers ended the series with 824 runs in eight innings at an average of 137.33, his journey from under-fire batsman to global superstar signed and sealed in just a few weeks.

With much less international cricket in those days, and with the Caribbean season finishing in the English spring, Sobers spent much of 1958 playing for Radcliffe in the Central Lancashire League, thereby following in Worrell's footsteps. The Lancashire leagues gave overseas players a living in the English summer before county cricket opened its doors to them in the late 1960s. Sobers had five seasons at Radcliffe and enjoyed his time there enormously. However, it coincided with the most painful event of his life: the death of his closest friend, the West Indian batsman Collie Smith.

Born in Jamaica and three years older than Sobers, the immensely popular Smith seemed destined for greatness as an attacking batsman and off-spinner. He'd scored a century on Test debut at his home ground against Australia in 1955, and Sobers felt that he could have become the better all-rounder. While Sobers shone at Radcliffe, Smith sparkled at their Lancashire league rivals Burnley, and in September 1959 they met up one night with Tom Dewdney – a Jamaican who'd opened the attack with Roy Gilchrist during the 365 match – after their respective league fixtures. Gilchrist was supposed to join them as they drove to London for a charity match, but, after waiting around for an hour or so, they gave up and left. The three men shared driving duties into the early hours and Sobers had just taken the wheel as they travelled along the A34 near Stone in Staffordshire. As he neared a bend, Sobers remembered being confronted by two dazzling headlights before ploughing head-on into a ten-ton cattle truck. He suffered a cut eye, a dislocated bone in his wrist and a severed nerve in one of his fingers. Dewdney was screaming hysterically in pain but Smith, who'd been asleep on the back seat, initially seemed unhurt. He told Sobers: "I'm alright, mun – go look after the big boy [Dewdney]". But Smith had damaged his spinal cord and died in hospital three days later. Sobers was charged with driving without due care and attention and fined £10, adding to the agony he already felt. He called it "the saddest episode" of his life, something that "has been on my conscience ever since" and, for the rest of his career, said that he was playing for two men – himself and Collie Smith.

Sobers's great friend Collie Smith acknowledges the applause for his second innings hundred against England at Trent Bridge in 1957.

In that devastating autumn of 1959, Sobers sank into deep depression. He sought comfort in alcohol and hit the bottle so hard it was as if he was trying to destroy himself. "Sometimes I would drink from one day to the next without even sleeping," he said. "Scotch or brandy, whatever was there." A few months later, in February 1960, Sobers returned to the scene of his 365 at Smith's home ground of Sabina Park. He felt "a lot of apprehension" and was worried how the crowd would react. "I couldn't have been more mistaken in my fears," he said. "The Jamaican public understood the grief I felt and mourned with me." Sobers paid tribute to his dear friend by scoring 147 against Peter May's England, having struck 226 in the First Test in Barbados. Sabina Park was Sobers's most successful Test ground in the Caribbean, and the only one anywhere on which he scored over 1,000 Test runs. In 11 Tests and 18 innings there, Sobers hit 1,354 runs at 104.15, with five centuries and four fifties. "The wicket at Sabina Park was not everyone's favourite, but it was good to me," he said.

Although Sobers stopped short of disappearing "into the mists of an alcoholic haze" after Smith's tragic death, he always enjoyed the game's social side and a good night out in the proper sense. Sobers's attitude – heightened by tragedy – was "live for today". Sometimes he burnt the candle at both ends and could survive on just four or five hours' sleep. "My view about sleep is that you go to bed when you are tired," he said. "If you still have plenty of energy to burn, you burn it." Sobers burnt it in an era long before today's obsession with sports science and nutrition. He played hard on the field and even harder off it, believing it inspired him to greater endeavour. Sobers cited his unbeaten 150 against

England at Lord's in 1973 as a classic example. At the end of day one, with West Indies 335 for four and Sobers 31 not out, team-mate Clive Lloyd suggested a night out. They visited some of Lloyd's friends and then Sobers met up with Reg Scarlett, a former West Indian off-spinner, who lived in London. Sobers stayed out all night, had no sleep and woke himself up with a cold shower before returning to the ground. When his score was 70, he felt churning pains in his stomach and he retired hurt to go to the toilet. Suitably relieved – and suitably refreshed by a couple of brandy and ports in the dressing-room too – Sobers resumed his innings when the next wicket fell. "Goodness me," said John Arlott on the radio. "West Indies 604 for seven – and here comes Sobers…"

Sobers hits out during his brandy and port fuelled innings of 150 not out against England at Lord's in 1973. Wicketkeeper Alan Knott looks on.

Sobers's sociability – and willingness to stand a round – made him great company with team-mates and opponents. He had a natural affinity with his fellow players and did not discriminate between their abilities. David Lloyd, the ex-Lancashire and England batsman-turned-commentator, said: "He was a gent, Garry. He knew how good he was, and he had a great respect for the game and for the people he played against. I've never, ever heard a bad word about Garry Sobers from anybody, and he took everybody to the cleaners."

The word genius is nowadays bandied like cheap confetti but, by common consent, Sobers was one and the greatest cricketer the world has seen. Born with two extra fingers that were later removed, as if there was something otherworldly about him from the start, he could literally do everything – bat with style and swashbuckling grace, bowl left-arm fast and seam the new ball, and back-of-the-hand spin with the old ball too. He was a brilliant fielder in any position. "No player has proven versatility of skill as convincingly as Sobers has done, effortlessly, and after the manner born," wrote Neville Cardus. He added that Sobers's secret was "power of relaxation and the gift of holding himself in reserve", saying: "Nobody has seen Sobers obviously in labour. He makes a stroke with moments to spare. His fastest ball – and it can be very fast – is bowled as though he could, with physical pressure, have bowled it a shade faster. He can, in the slips, catch the lightning snick with the grace and nonchalance of Hammond himself. The sure sign of mastery, of genius of any order, is absence of strain, natural freedom of rhythm."

With his long-sleeved shirt and upturned collar, Sobers was instantly identifiable, a charismatic magnet for hero worship. "He came through the pavilion gate like the Great Gatsby gliding into a black-tie ball," wrote the author Duncan Hamilton. Sobers's achievements will always echo: he was the first man to hit six sixes in an over, off the Glamorgan left-armer Malcolm Nash for Nottinghamshire at Swansea in 1968, while Bradman always reckoned that Sobers's 254 for the World XI against Australia at Melbourne in 1972 was "probably the greatest exhibition of batting ever seen in Australia". Sobers considered his unbeaten 163 against England at Lord's in 1966 his "most satisfying innings", along with the aforementioned 150 at the same venue seven years later, powered by brandy and port and a sleepless night. "The innings which always pleased me were those where I had to play in a restrained way, when I had to

Sobers holds aloft a Barbados Tridents jersey bearing the legend "365" before a match in the 2014 Caribbean Premier League.

play in conditions which suited the fielding side. I was less satisfied with innings on good pitches when the batting side had all the advantages."

By that yardstick, the 365 was not quite on the same plane of personal satisfaction, although it was the most famous innings he ever played. Sobers bemoaned how the press would always contact him whenever someone threatened to topple it. "Every time anyone went past 250 anywhere in the world, I would take telephone calls asking me how I felt about my record being under threat. Records are made to be broken; that's what they are for. I remember when Graham Gooch scored 333 [for England against India at Lord's in 1990]. It was lucky that I was on the golf course as the English press tried to telephone me every few runs to ask me what I thought. I tried to tell them it didn't mean that much but I don't think they believed me. They kept calling back until Graham lost his wicket 32 runs short."

Of the 365, Sobers said: "That innings didn't change me as a person, but it changed my life. From that moment on, I was instantly recognised throughout the Caribbean and the cricketing world. It did not alter my bank balance. There were no bonuses in those days."

West Indies v Pakistan

Played at Sabina Park, Kingston, Jamaica, on 26, 27, 28 February, 1, 3, 4 March, 1958.
Toss: Pakistan. Result: West Indies won by an innings and 174 runs.

PAKISTAN

Hanif Mohammad c Alexander b Gilchrist	3	–	b Gilchrist	13
†Imtiaz Ahmed c Alexander b Gilchrist	122	–	lbw b Dewdney	0
Saeed Ahmed c Weekes b Smith	52	–	c Gilchrist b Gibbs	44
W. Mathias b Dewdney	77	–	c Alexander b Atkinson	19
Alimuddin c Alexander b Atkinson	15	–	b Gibbs	30
*A. H. Kardar c Sobers b Atkinson	15	–	(7) lbw b Dewdney	57
Wazir Mohammad c Walcott b Dewdney	2	–	(6) lbw b Atkinson	106
Fazal Mahmood c Alexander b Atkinson	6	–	c Alexander b Atkinson	0
Nasim-ul-Ghani b Atkinson	5	–	absent hurt	
Mahmood Hussain b Atkinson	20	–	absent hurt	
Khan Mohammad not out	3	–	(9) not out	0
Lb 5, nb 3	8		B 16, lb 3	19

1/4 (1) 2/122 (3) 3/223 (2)   (102 overs) 328   1/8 (2) 2/20 (1)   (96.3 overs) 288
4/249 (5) 5/287 (4) 6/291 (6)   3/57 (4) 4/105 (3)
7/299 (8) 8/301 (7) 9/317 (9) 10/328 (10)   5/120 (5) 6/286 (6) 7/286 (8) 8/288 (7)

Gilchrist 25–3–106–2; Dewdney 26–4–88–2; Atkinson 21–7–42–5; Gibbs 7–0–32–0;
Smith 18–3–39–1; Sobers 5–1–13–0. *Second innings* – Gilchrist 12–3–65–1;
Dewdney 19.3–2–51–2; Atkinson 18–6–36–3; Gibbs 21–6–46–2; Smith 8–2–20–0;
Sobers 15–4–41–0; Weekes 3–1–10–0.

WEST INDIES

C. C. Hunte run out (sub Ijaz Butt)	260	C. L. Walcott not out	88
R. B. Kanhai c Imtiaz Ahmed			
b Fazal Mahmood	25	B 2, lb 7, w 4	13
G. S. Sobers not out	365		
E. D. Weekes c Hanif Mohammad		1/87 (2) (3 wkts dec, 208.1 overs) 790	
b Fazal Mahmood	39	2/533 (1) 3/602 (4)	

O. G. Smith, *†F. C. M. Alexander, E. S. Atkinson, L. R. Gibbs, R. Gilchrist and
D. T. Dewdney did not bat.

Mahmood Hussain 0.5–0–2–0; Fazal Mahmood 85.2–20–247–2; Khan Mohammad
54–5–259–0; Nasim-ul-Ghani 15–3–39–0; Kardar 37–2–141–0; Mathias 4–0–20–0;
Alimuddin 4–0–34–0; Hanif Mohammad 2–0–11–0; Saeed Ahmed 6–0–24–0.

Umpires: R. C. Burke and T. A. Ewart.

9

Brian Lara (375)
West Indies versus England
Antigua 1994

Garry Sobers didn't think that his record would be broken. "The modern era of limited-overs cricket produces batsmen who don't really have the ability to bat a long time," he said in the early 1990s. However, it wasn't long before Sobers had cause to change his mind. In April 1994, his 365 was finally beaten after 36 years – the longest gap between the torch changing hands – when Brian Lara made 375 for West Indies against England in Antigua. Ever since Lara scored 277 on only his fifth Test appearance against Australia in Sydney the previous year, Sobers had pronounced him the likeliest to take his crown. He'd even playfully admonished him for missing the chance that time when, within touching distance of turning his maiden Test hundred into a triple, as Sobers had, Lara was run out contemplating a risky single. After Lara beat him in Antigua, Sobers said that he was "the only person playing who could have beaten my record", and that "Lara is the only batsman playing the game today who plays the game the way it should be played".

A cricketer after his own heart, then, one who saw it as his duty to entertain the crowds, Lara first met Sobers in 1987. He was brought over from his native Trinidad to take part in the inaugural Sir Garfield Sobers International Schools

Cricket Tournament as a 17-year-old. "When I shook hands, Brian could scarcely speak," said Sobers. "He just kept repeating, 'You're Sir Sobers! You're Sir Sobers!'" But when the tiny, tongue-tied Lara picked up a bat, Sobers straightaway recognised greatness. "I could see all the technique and all the ability. He could hardly knock the ball off the square, but they couldn't get him out." Sobers became "his biggest advocate", pushing for Lara's inclusion for West Indies long before he was actually picked. He was just "so naturally talented", he felt, "a real West Indian batsman in the time-honoured tradition". Over time, their bond developed; Sobers related to the pressures experienced by Lara (fame, jealousy, colossal expectations) and Lara rang him for batting advice. He said of Sobers: "He's someone who believed in me from a very early age... He had strong feelings about my ability to play the game at the highest level."

Brian Lara began playing almost before he'd learned to walk. His elder brother, Randolph, made him a wooden bat when he was three. Echoing the young Don Bradman with his golf ball, water tank and cricket stump, the young Lara spent hours hitting a marble against the garage wall using a stick or a broom handle. Each time he missed the rebounding object it classed as a wicket, yet still these private matches lasted for days. A tailender on the family scorecard (Lara was the tenth of 11 children), he was enrolled at the local cricket coaching clinic, aged six. His sister, Agnes, had spotted an advert seeking cricket-mad youngsters and she bought him a green cap, a proper bat and some white clothes especially. From then on, his father, Bunty, became his biggest supporter, never missing a match or a practice session. Tragically, he never saw Brian play for the West Indies, suffering a fatal heart attack during a Test match against India at Trinidad in 1989 when his son was 12th man. It was another 20 months before Lara made his Test debut, against Pakistan in Lahore. He scored 44 in the first innings and was the last of leg-spinner Abdul Qadir's 236 Test wickets.

Since his 277 in Sydney had shot him to international fame, Lara had struggled to repeat such form. Going into the five-Test series against England in 1994, he'd made three half-centuries in his next nine Test innings, with a highest of 96 against Pakistan in Trinidad. After 11 Tests, that Sydney epic remained a statistical outlier. Like Sobers heading into the 1957-58 Pakistan series, hundreds were uppermost in Lara's mind, his target for the year "to get a few centuries, maybe a double and even a triple". On paper, England's visit presented him with an ideal chance. Michael Atherton led a young and inexperienced team and was himself a young and inexperienced captain, having been appointed, aged 25, after Graham Gooch's resignation the previous year. Victory in

Brian Lara is run out for 277 against Australia in Sydney, the innings that shot him to international stardom.

Atherton's second Test in charge, the sixth and last of the 1993 Ashes, ended a sorry sequence in which England had gone ten games and 13 months without a Test win (it was their first Test win against Australia for seven years). Convinced that something had to change, specifically an end to a closed-shop mentality and a reluctance to blood young players, Atherton gave youth its head on the West Indies trip. Gone were the "Three Gs", Messrs Gooch, Gower and Gatting, to be replaced by young batsmen such as Nasser Hussain, Graham Thorpe and Mark Ramprakash – "street fighters," said Atherton, "with plenty of spunk". Atherton wanted cricketers who would not be scarred by previous meetings with the West Indies and who could grow in the way that Australia's had under Allan Border. "Australia and Allan Border were my role models," he said, Border having taken his team from the doldrums in the mid-1980s on a journey that would see them supplant the West Indies as the game's No. 1. In 1994, West Indies were still clinging to that status despite the retirements of several great players. The greatest of them, the batting genius Viv Richards, had played his last Test two and a half years earlier, with fast bowler Malcolm Marshall and wicketkeeper Jeffrey Dujon also bowing out in that same Oval Test of 1991. A few months earlier, Gordon Greenidge, the powerful opening batsman, had also exited stage left, having featured in two decades of West Indian dominance. West Indies went into the 1994 series having won 12 and drawn two of their previous 14 home series dating back to Sobers's last in 1974.

With few expecting much from Atherton's side (the average age of his squad was 26, with only Alec Stewart, Devon Malcolm, Jack Russell and Robin Smith 30 or above), Lara sensed that his time had come. But he missed another chance for a hundred in the first Test in Jamaica. After England scored 234, collapsing from 121 without loss after a fine stand between Atherton and Stewart, Lara was bowled for 83 by the occasional off-spin of Graeme Hick, whose Test batting and bowling averages would finish the wrong way round – 31 with the bat, 56 with the ball. *Wisden* felt that Lara "played strokes well worth the price of admission", helping West Indies to 407 and a lead of 173. Hick top-scored with 96 as England replied with 267, Lara one of two men out as the hosts cruised to a 95-run target.

In the second game in Guyana, Lara finally got his second Test century, scoring 167 in an innings win. "Lara's control was hypnotic, his timing and placement stunning," said *Wisden*. "England were grateful to remove him for as little as 167." Lara had a quiet homecoming in the Third Test in Trinidad, scoring 43 and 12 as England were dismissed for 46 in pursuit of 194 to lose the series. Curtly Ambrose, the 6ft 7in fast bowler, took six for 24 in one of the all-time great spells, England narrowly avoiding their lowest Test total of 45 against Australia at Sydney in 1887. A humiliating defeat to a West Indies Board XI followed before England arrived for the Fourth Test in Barbados, where no visiting Test team had won for 59 years. Under the circumstances, 3–0 down and having just been routed for 46, England's 208-run victory – inspired by twin centuries from Stewart and eight first-innings wickets from the Middlesex seamer Angus Fraser – was one of sport's great comebacks. Lara scored 26 in the first innings and top-scored with 64 in the second, one of five wickets for Somerset pace bowler Andrew Caddick. Lara's dismissal – caught by the Middlesex left-arm spinner Phil Tufnell at mid-on off a mistimed hook – was branded careless and irresponsible by the Caribbean press. The criticism stung and only increased his determination to finish the series strongly in the last Test in Antigua. England were unchanged, but West Indies were without their captain, Richie Richardson, and vice-captain, Desmond Haynes, who had hamstring and finger injuries respectively. The hosts handed a debut to Stuart Williams, a 24-year-old attacking batsman from Nevis, and recalled to open with him the 30-year-old Phil Simmons, who'd been dropped after the First Test. Fast bowler Courtney Walsh took over as captain, with Lara serving as vice.

On a warm and sunny morning, Williams and Simmons fell inside the first 40 minutes as West Indies slipped to 12 for two after winning the toss. Williams was caught hooking at long leg by Caddick off Fraser, and Simmons trapped lbw by Caddick, England starting the match with the same buoyancy with which they ended the Barbados Test. Jack Russell, the England wicketkeeper, said: "I started thinking, 'This is going all right. We'll knock this lot over and won't be out here for too long.'" But Lara and Jimmy Adams had other ideas. Initially, the third-wicket pair were circumspect, like young chicks taking their first tentative steps away from the nest. Lara laboured over an hour for his first ten runs and had only 23 at lunch out of 48 for two from 28 overs. Adams, a willowy left-hander, and a year older than Lara at 25, had scored 11 at the break in 82 minutes. Then, after "an almost strokeless first session", and with the stadium "packed beyond capacity", the writer Tony Becca said that West Indies' fans were "lifted to heights of ecstasy by strokes which sparkled in the brilliant afternoon sun". Lara pulled a short ball from Tufnell for four and followed up with three successive boundaries off all-rounder Chris Lewis, "the little man leaning on his bat," wrote Becca, "as the cheers rang around the ground as if to say, 'What extravagance should I perpetrate next?'" At tea, the total had shot up to 166 for two (Lara 92, Adams 54), Lara soon going to his third Test hundred with another pulled boundary off Tufnell. Whereas his first fifty had come from 121 balls, Lara's second had arrived in just 59 deliveries.

As if to reflect his now carefree progress, mirroring the carefree mood in the stands, Lara dispensed with his grille-less helmet and batted instead in his West Indies cap. This reflected also the gentle nature of England's attack, shorn of its most potent weapon in the Derbyshire fast bowler Devon Malcolm. The 30-year-old played in the opening Test but suffered a knee injury and had to return to England for treatment. Although he subsequently rejoined the tour, Malcolm wasn't risked in the remaining Tests, England relying on Fraser and Caddick with support from Lewis and the spinners. Fraser, 28, bowled with control throughout the series while Caddick, 25, showed rich potential – not least with second-innings returns of six for 65 in Trinidad and five for 63 in Barbados. Lewis, 25, was a mercurial figure. The Nottinghamshire all-rounder ran into trouble with the England management early in the trip when he shaved his head – Malcolm acting as barber – and got sunstroke, causing him to miss a match. The journalist Simon Barnes called it "the most idiotic cricket injury of all time", while *The Sun* labelled Lewis "the prat without a hat". Although Lewis played in all five Tests, his returns were disappointing (170 runs at 21.25, 14 wickets at 39.50). Atherton observed: "Like every other captain in the last decade, I fancied my chances of getting the best out of the enigmatic Lewis, and like every other captain I failed. In the end, you can only lead a player to the well; you can't drink the water for him." After his side's wicketless afternoon in Antigua, Atherton could celebrate only one more breakthrough on the opening evening, Adams caught by substitute fielder Nasser Hussain off Fraser for 59, ending a stand with Lara of 179.

Lara then shared 81 with Keith Arthurton, a dashing 29-year-old left-hander, as West Indies reached 274 for three at stumps. On a marble-top pitch that gave nothing to the bowlers, many sensed that Lara's innings could be special. The man himself reflected: "It was only after the first day's play, when I was on 164, that I thought it might be a big innings, maybe a world record." Lara thought his score would already have been bigger but for "long, coarse grass over much of the outfield".

After batting for almost the whole day, Lara went to bed earlier than usual. He woke at 5.30am and played nine holes of golf to settle his nerves. "I felt a lot of tension and I thought I needed to relax." In warm sunshine, he resumed his innings carefully, playing out two maidens from Fraser before pulling Caddick to the boundary – his first scoring shot of day two. Lewis was dispatched to the point fence and later worked for a leg-side single that raised Lara's 200, a milestone celebrated with a perfunctory punch of triumph as if to conserve energy for further rejoicing. Arthurton, batting with a damaged hand that limited his strokeplay, was caught behind off Caddick just after lunch, having scored 47 and added 183 for the fourth wicket. Lara now played with growing panache, Tony Becca writing that "the left-handed genius from Santa Cruz batted in the manner of a millionaire spreading his strokes like largesse for the enjoyment of his subjects". Becca said that Lara "went around the compass with a diadem of strokes – hooking and pulling, driving and cutting with an arrogance which reminded of Richards, the old master beaming with satisfaction from the press box when the new master leaned into a Chris Lewis half-volley and smashed it to the extra-cover boundary".

After Richards's retirement, the Caribbean craved a new batting monarch. It was soon a case of "The king is dead, long live the king!" as Lara answered the burning need. Whereas Richards frightened simply by his walk to the wicket, slowly windmilling powerful arms while chewing gum menacingly, Lara terrified more through a towering backlift that brought the blade down like the snap of a guillotine. At its height as the ball was delivered, Lara's bat resembled a periscope that shot down quickly from whence it came, as if to avoid enemy detection. Although relatively small at 5ft 8in, the momentum gave him great power, helped by fast hands and supple wrists redolent of a reggae drummer. Among the glories of Lara's repertoire were a whipped pull and a late cut that revealed the heart of an artist. Like Richards he was cool and charismatic, the cynosure of enraptured crowds. Like Richards too, he could pickpocket a game away in an eye-blink, leaving no clue but the trail of his runs.

At lunch, when Lara's score was 225, talk of a record had started to spread. No one sensed it more than Sobers, who was present as part of a series of events to mark the 40th anniversary of his Test debut against Len Hutton's England. While accepting a plaque during the lunch break and a cheque for $US5,000 on behalf of his cricket fund from Lester Bird, the prime minister of Antigua and Barbuda, Sobers spoke briefly. "I don't want to be long because I know you want to see a young man – a young man of quality and promise – get past 365," he said. "In fact, I would like to see it also, and I wish him good luck in his quest. He is a great little player, but then you have to be to score like that." Sobers reinforced his message during a flying visit to the West Indies dressing room, telling Lara that if he kept his head down, the record would be his. Sobers's words meant much to a man whose beaming smile and boyish exuberance made light of the mountainous challenge ahead.

Such was Lara's scoring rate, he was odds-on to break the record if still batting at stumps on day two, but three rain delays stole 23 overs and cost him the chance. The delays disturbed his concentration and he was grateful for the steadying influence of Shivnarine Chanderpaul, his 19-year-old batting partner, whom he praised for showing invaluable maturity. Chanderpaul, a crabby left-hander playing his fourth Test, quietly urged him on, helping to wear down England on a day when they claimed only Arthurton's wicket. While Chanderpaul dropped anchor, Lara set sail, reaching his 250 with a pulled boundary off Tufnell and then steering beyond his career-best 277 against Australia in Sydney. On 286, Lara played what he considered his first false shot, edging Caddick not far from wicketkeeper Russell. Chanderpaul walked down and whispered some Mother Mary-like words of wisdom. "I shall always be grateful to him for the part he played in my success," said Lara.

Five runs later and Lara equalled Viv Richards's 291 against England at The Oval in 1976. That innings was the icing on the cake of a series in which Richards scored 829 runs in four Tests at 118.42 to help West Indies to a 3–0 win after England captain Tony Greig infamously pledged to "make them grovel". Richards missed the chance to beat Sobers when bowled aiming a tired shot at Greig having been kept up by well-wishers in his hotel room to celebrate his 200 the previous day. Not that Richards was thinking about "cracking any kind of record", as he put it. "If my cricket ever gets to that state, I'd chuck it right away," he said. It was when Lara drew level with Richards's score that Atherton took out a slip for the first time, only for Lara to nick Caddick's next ball through the vacant gap. "He could quite conceivably have been taking the mickey," said Atherton, who added that "I wouldn't know because the scale of his talent was way outside my understanding". Lara soon steered Caddick through backward point for two to reach 300, the crowd spilling on to the field and one spectator grabbing him round the waist and hoisting him in the air.

Lara was only the third West Indian after Sobers and Lawrence Rowe to score a Test triple-hundred. Rowe, an elegant right-hander from Jamaica, and a brilliant exponent of the hook and pull, made 302 against England at Barbados in 1974. He also missed the chance to beat Sobers – who registered a duck in the same innings – when seventh out after opening the batting, caught at deep midwicket off Greig. Rowe's was one of five triple-centuries in Test cricket between those of Sobers and Lara, a list headed by Graham Gooch's 333 for England against India at Lord's in 1990. With the record in sight, Gooch was bowled aiming what he termed a "lazy, airy sort of drive" at new-ball bowler Manoj Prabhakar. The Essex man's disappointment was softened by another hundred in the second innings (123), which gave him a record aggregate in a Test of 456. Prior to Gooch, Bobby Simpson scored 311 for Australia in the Old Trafford Ashes Test of 1964; John Edrich struck 310 not out for England against New Zealand at Headingley the following year (Mike Smith's declaration denied him the chance to go for the record), and Bob Cowper made 307 for Australia against England at Melbourne in 1966. At stumps on day two in Antigua, Lara had 320 out of 502 for four and now stood eighth on the all-time list.

That night, the 24-year-old experienced the same tension to which Sobers and Hutton freely admitted. He woke at 4am with his hands sweating and his heart pounding. "My mind was churning over what it would mean to me if I managed to score 46 more runs," he said. "My whole life flashed through my mind. I thought of all the people who had faith in me. I knew I couldn't let them down." Lara ruled out another early-morning round of golf and despite having been awake for several hours, almost missed the team bus in his frazzled condition. When he got to the ground, he sat in the dressing-room fighting back tears, memories of his late father returning to mind. "I knew he was willing me on to this historic landmark."

Forty-six more runs... the same number for which the entire England team had been dismissed in the Third Test in Trinidad. Forty-six more runs... the sort of figure that seems ostensibly straightforward for a man who already has 320 and yet, amid the enormity of the occasion, about as straightforward as trying to repel Curtly Ambrose on that devastating day in Port-of-Spain. Lara began the third day skittishly, which dawned with barely a cloud in the sky. There were nervy prods and panicky singles, Christopher Martin-Jenkins observing in the *Daily Telegraph* that "the brief signs of human frailty only added to the already piquant tension". Never was that tension more evident than when a remarkable thing happened when Lara had 347. He played and missed at a ball from Fraser that leapt and left him, the first time in 12 hours' batting he'd been genuinely beaten. "Arsey bastard," quipped Fraser, or, as Martin-Jenkins beyond earshot in the press box interpreted, the bowler "towering benignly over the young tormentor, like an uncle talking to a precocious nephew". Fraser, his words laced with irony, knew there was no point sledging Lara. "He was too good a player to sledge. You were wasting your time. It all comes down to who has the biggest gun and you don't have it, so you just sometimes have to accept you are playing against somebody bigger and better than you are." The respect was mutual. "I have always had great admiration for Angus Fraser," wrote Lara. "He is a slower, less menacing version of Curtly Ambrose, but brings the ball down from a considerable height and pitches it on a line and length that batsmen are not happy with." As the tension built like a Hitchcock thriller – *Vertigo*, perhaps, considering the high numbers involved – Lara jokingly complained to Atherton that he was making things hard for him, the England captain drying up singles in a desperate effort to keep him off strike.

Lara drives during the 375.

The stands were now awash with colour, the ground a swaying mass of noise. It was a Monday, a work day, but it seemed as if every Antiguan was inside a ground that held around 12,000 people, some watching from precarious vantage points as they had when Sobers took the record in 1958. Two of the "The Rec's" great characters, Gravy and Mayfield, were in full voice at opposite ends of the venue, trying to outdo each other with improvised dance moves. Gravy was dressed as Father Christmas, while Mayfield had a pile of old vinyl records ready to smash in celebration if Lara could break the record that mattered. Another of "The Rec's" great stalwarts, DJ "Chickie", had spectators dancing to various tunes as a metal band drummed out matching rhythms. The atmosphere was a strange mix of premature ecstasy and pent-up anxiety, the party already in full swing even though everyone was crossing their fingers that Lara would not unwittingly switch off the lights and sound system, as it were, by losing his wicket.

After that play-and-miss at Fraser, which caused one or two hearts to skip a beat, Lara took Lewis for a leg-side single to reach his 350. By now, every run was greeted with delirious cheers – and not just inside the Recreation Ground. With people able to follow Lara's progress on television and radio around the world, including on Sky TV and BBC *Test Match Special* in England, this was the first time that pursuit of Test cricket's greatest individual batting record had felt like a truly global experience. That was not the case in Sobers's day and, having bemoaned how the press would always ring him whenever anyone threatened to beat the 365, there was no need now to alert him to the fact. He was still there in person, glued to the entertainment having stayed on after the previous day's celebrations to mark his Test debut.

By the time that Lara had 361, one hit away from equalling the record, the 57-year-old Sobers had been ushered down to the boundary edge, his own nerves jangling as much as his protégé's. In readiness for the anticipated pitch invasion, a hundred or so policemen – dressed in marl-grey shirts and black hats – ringed the boundary as Planet Cricket held its breath. Then Caddick came steaming in again and Lara, with a daring that made a mockery of the moment, lashed as sweet a cover-drive as he can ever have lashed, the ball racing to the boundary to tie the record. After a quick and calming word from Chanderpaul, followed by a firm glove-punch, Lara was back on strike in the next over to face Lewis. At 11.47am Eastern Caribbean Time precisely, with a smiling Atherton a picture of sportsmanship as he walked in from his fielding position, Lewis bowled a bouncer which Lara's periscope backlift seized on instantly as he pulled the ball out towards the square-leg boundary.

> *"He's gone for a pull!" exclaimed the former England captain Bob Willis on Sky. "And there it is! Brian Lara's done it! The ball rockets into the boundary fence. The new world record holder is Brian Charles Lara of Trinidad and Tobago. [Pause.] What a moment for Trinidad and Tobago and West Indies cricket."*

Unbeknown to Willis and the watching millions, Lara, in playing the shot, had brushed the off stump with his right leg. The off bail jumped up but, incredibly, it stayed on the stump as if a divine hand had reached down to stop it from falling. Jack Russell was relieved that he didn't have to appeal. "I thought to myself that if I do, I won't make it home. I'll be lynched. The bail didn't fall off in the end but it stayed slightly out of its slot." No sooner had Lara sent the

The off bail jumps up but, incredibly, stays on the stump as Lara pulls the historic boundary that takes him past Sobers.

ball crashing into the advertising hoardings than fans spilled on from all directions. The police presence proved about as effective as a chocolate fireguard in preventing the flames of adulation from engulfing him, Martin-Jenkins writing that it was unclear whether the police were "more concerned to protect Lara or to congratulate him themselves". Amid the bedlam, Sobers, grey-haired and bespectacled, emerged Mandela-like on to the outfield as iconic images of the new and old record-holder were beamed across the world. Initially, Sobers had to wait to congratulate him due to the swarm of well-wishers. Eventually, a path was cleared as if Moses had parted the Red Sea. The cricketers embraced, Sobers's joy evident as they shared one of sport's most touching moments. Lara said: "He clasped me and said how very proud he was. 'I'm very happy for you. I knew you could do it, son. You were always the one.'" Finally, Sobers and Lara loosened their grip and Lara instinctively fell to his knees. He kissed the pitch to complete celebrations that lasted for a good ten minutes. In echoes of the crowd invasion at Sabina Park in 1958, when the pitch was damaged and Sobers denied the chance to bat on towards 400, the Australian umpire Darrell Hair accosted one man who charged towards the wicket in Antigua with menacing mien. It turned out to be George, the groundsman, who was also endeavouring to protect his pride and joy.

When the field was eventually cleared, Lewis asked for the ball back. Amazingly, despite the hundreds of people who'd rushed on, it was still resting against the boundary board where Lara's shot had left it. He added six more runs and then got an outside edge to an attempted drive off Caddick and was caught behind by Russell, tumbling to his left. His 375 had come from 538 balls in 12 hours, 46 minutes and included 99

Lara and Sobers share a joke when the drama is over.

singles, 33 twos, 10 threes and 45 fours. As Lara walked off, Caddick called out to halt him and generously shook his hand, Lara then exiting through a tunnel of bats held up by team-mates. Later, he told reporters: "It was an unbelievable feeling, going past such a record, set way before I was born. It's going to take a long time to realise what I've achieved. I'll have to live up to what I've done. A lot of people will be expecting a lot and I can't disappoint them. I just wish my father was here to see me; he was my biggest inspiration." West Indies declared on 593 for five when Lara was out (Chanderpaul finishing on 75), England also scoring 593 thanks to centuries from Atherton and Robin Smith, who shared 303 for the third wicket. West Indies were 43 for nought in their second innings when hands were shaken on the draw.

Lara was leading run-scorer in the series with 798 at 99.75, over twice as many as West Indies' next-highest scorer Jimmy Adams (374). Atherton was England's best batsman with 510 at 56.67, closely followed by Stewart (477 at 53.00). Atherton's captaincy was commended by *Wisden*, who said that he "returned home from what remained an emphatic defeat with his reputation enhanced". Lara returned home to a hero's welcome. The government of Trinidad gave him land for a house, a new street was named Brian Lara Promenade and he received the island's highest honour, the Trinity Cross, as well as the key to the city of Port-of-Spain. Lara also received a motorcade tour of the island and was feted by scores of schoolchildren who'd been given the day off. Commercial benefits – which came from all directions – included free air travel and telephone time.

Nine days after the 375, barely enough time to drink it all in, Lara landed at Heathrow to take up a contract with

Warwickshire. It was the next chapter in a barely believable story in which he became – starting with the 375 – the first man to score seven hundreds in eight first-class innings, culminating in a world-record 501 not out against Durham at Edgbaston. Lara's scores in this 52-day period were: 375, 147, 106, 120 not out, 136, 26, 140 and 501 not out. The 501 beat Hanif Mohammad's 499 for Karachi against Bahawalpur at Karachi in 1959 and came after Lara was bowled on ten by a no-ball from Anderson Cummins, his West Indies team-mate and 12th man during the 375 match, and also dropped on 18 by wicketkeeper Chris Scott off left-arm pace bowler Simon Brown. "Jeez, I hope he doesn't go on and get a hundred," said Scott. Remarkably, Bob Woolmer, the former Kent and England batsman, and Warwickshire's coach that summer, had seen Hanif's 499 and is thought to be the only person who saw that and Lara's quintuple-century. As a ten-year-old at prep school in Tonbridge, Woolmer had been flown out to Karachi where his father was working. The journey was a story in itself. Woolmer's plane was forced down en route by fighters in Baghdad and the young boy felt "very scared". After that, the gentle machinations of the Quaid-e-Azam Trophy, Pakistan's domestic tournament, must have seemed like a blessed relief for the young Woolmer, whose father dropped him at the ground before going to work. "There was a big crowd, a matting wicket, a very rough outfield and a bloke getting run out," he said. "My father asked me what happened and I said, 'Well, someone got 499, dad.'" During Lara's 501, Woolmer remembered: "At lunch, Brian said to me, 'What score's the first-class record?' I said, '499. You're not going for that?' He said, 'Well, are you thinking of declaring?' And Dermot Reeve said, 'Well, sort of. We'll see how it goes.'

So it was agreed he could at least go for the Warwickshire record 305, and I said to Dermot, 'Let him go the whole way.' He was just so single-minded, it was always inevitable, almost mystical.'"

Mushtaq Mohammad, Hanif's brother, who played in the 499 game, was working in Birmingham just down the road. He received a phone call alerting him to what was afoot when Lara passed 450. He dashed to the ground but got there too late. When news of the record falling reached Hanif, he paid Lara this tribute: "He's very short, and many other short Test players have scored lots of runs, like me, Sir Don Bradman and Sir Len Hutton." Whereas Hanif was run out off the penultimate ball of a day's play, expecting an overnight declaration, Lara reached his 500 from the penultimate ball of the match, crashing the very occasional

Forty-nine days after setting the new Test record, Lara poses in front of an Edgbaston scoreboard proclaiming his first-class record 501.

bowling of batsman John Morris to the cover boundary. It was just two months since the publication of the 1994 *Wisden* and yet, astonishingly, its two greatest batting records were out of date. "The 501 was different in so many respects," said Lara. "The pitch was not quite so good but the outfield was faster. And obviously Durham's attack wasn't anywhere near as good as England's. It was unbelievable that both records should be broken in such a short space of time. The 375 was more important because it was in a Test match, but I will cherish both records. Test cricket is the highest form of cricket, and to have broken the record of Sir Garfield Sobers in a Test in the West Indies meant more to me than anything I had achieved before."

For years, Sobers's 365 had stood at the pinnacle. Then, on an Antigua island famous for its 365 beaches, it had gone to his protégé. "Records are made to be broken," said Sobers. "It had to go some day, and who better to do it than this guy. I am happy that he did it. No one can bat like him."

West Indies v England

Played at Antigua Recreation Ground, St John's, Antigua, on 16, 17, 18, 20, 21 April, 1994.
Toss: West Indies. Result: Match drawn.

WEST INDIES

P. V. Simmons lbw b Caddick	8	– not out	22
S. C. Williams c Caddick b Fraser	3	– not out	21
B. C. Lara c Russell b Caddick	375		
J. C. Adams c sub (N. Hussain) b Fraser	59		
K. L. T. Arthurton c Russell b Caddick	47		
S. Chanderpaul not out	75		
Lb 3, nb 23	26		

1/11 (2) 2/12 (1)   (5 wkts dec, 180.2 overs) 593   (no wkt, 24 overs) 43
3/191 (4) 4/374 (5) 5/593 (3)

†J. R. Murray, W. K. M. Benjamin, C. E. L. Ambrose, K. C. G. Benjamin and *C. A. Walsh did not bat.

Fraser 43–4–121–2; Caddick 47.2–8–158–3; Tufnell 39–8–110–0; Lewis 33–1–140–0; Hick 18–3–61–0. *Second innings* – Fraser 2–1–2–0; Caddick 2–1–11–0; Tufnell 6–4–5–0; Hick 8–2–11–0; Ramprakash 3–1–5–0; Thorpe 2–1–1–0; Stewart 1–0–8–0.

ENGLAND

*M. A. Atherton c Murray b Ambrose	135	A. R. C. Fraser b Adams	0
A. J. Stewart c Ambrose b K. C. G. Benjamin	24	P. C. R. Tufnell lbw b W. K. M. Benjamin	0
M. R. Ramprakash lbw b K. C. G. Benjamin	19		
R. A. Smith lbw b K. C. G. Benjamin	175		
G. A. Hick b K. C. G. Benjamin	20	B 9, lb 20, nb 23	52
G. P. Thorpe c Adams b Chanderpaul	9		
†R. C. Russell c Murray b W. K. M. Benjamin	62	1/40 (2) 2/70 (3) (206.1 overs) 593	
C. C. Lewis not out	75	3/373 (4) 4/393 (1)	
A. R. Caddick c W. K. M. Benjamin b Adams	22	5/401 (5) 6/417 (6) 7/535 (7)	
		8/585 (9) 9/589 (10) 10/593 (11)	

Ambrose 40–18–66–1; Walsh 40–9–123–0; W. K. M. Benjamin 41.1–15–93–2; K. C. G. Benjamin 37–7–110–4; Chanderpaul 24–1–94–1; Adams 22–4–74–2; Arthurton 2–1–4–0.

Umpires: S. A. Bucknor and D. B. Hair.

Referee: J. R. Reid.

10

Matthew Hayden (380)
Australia versus Zimbabwe
Perth 2003

A month before Brian Lara's 375, Australia handed a Test debut to a left-handed opener from the Queensland bush. Matthew Hayden, 22, was called up for the First Test against South Africa in Johannesburg after Mark Taylor fell ill on the morning of the match. Hayden was caught behind for 15 in the first innings off Allan Donald, who broke Hayden's thumb at the start of his second innings before Fanie de Villiers bowled him for five. South Africa won by 197 runs, Australia taking the Second Test in Cape Town by nine wickets ahead of a drawn decider in Durban. Hayden did not play another Test for nearly three years and only seven Tests in six years before sealing his place. Like Lara, who had to bide his time before breaking into the West Indies side of the early 1990s, so Hayden had to wait to become a regular in Australia's team. Unlike Lara, whose delayed entry was often attributed to the selectors' reluctance to change a winning side, Hayden's stop–start formative years were mainly due to misgivings concerning his technique – specifically, a tendency to play around his front pad/leg-side game. But three seasons of county cricket with Hampshire and Northamptonshire helped to turn a perceived weakness into a strength, Hayden coming to view his favourite shot as the back-foot force through the leg side.

"Force", in fact, was very much the word that applied to Hayden, who'd toured England in 1993 and scored over 1,000 first-class runs without playing in any of the six Tests. "Haydos", as he was nicknamed, was a man-mountain: tall, square-shouldered and phenomenally powerful, he bullied and intimidated opponents with his barrel-chested build and slightly contemptuous gum-chewing. One adversary likened playing against him to bowling at a sightscreen; he filled the crease in the way that Peter Schmeichel filled the Manchester United goal. Somewhere behind Hayden's broad bat and forearms the size of tree trunks, it was said, were the stumps, positively dwarfed by a man who puffed out his chest like a nightclub bouncer. But Hayden's strength was not just physical. Mentally he was tougher than the bushlands of his youth: intensely driven, fiercely determined, and inclined to

A young Matthew Hayden batting during the 1993 tour of England. He scored over 1,000 first-class runs on the trip but did not make his Test debut until a year later.

see setbacks as minor bumps. Like Lara, he perhaps sensed his destiny long before the doubting Thomases were convinced of it. In short, he had the make-up – if not the set aim – of someone who could break the world Test record.

Hayden, in fact, had little grasp of the game's history and was, in his own words, a "laid-back country kid" when he came on the scene. He'd grown up on his parents' peanut farm in Kingaroy, a two-and-a-half hour drive from Brisbane, where he'd learned his cricket in the backyard with older brother Gary. Whereas Gary, also his first coach, was a dab hand at leaving the ball, Matthew just liked to whack it. "He was always amazed at the way I just went out to hit the ball," he said. "I just wanted to bludgeon the ball everywhere." Hayden's mother was a drama teacher at the local state high school and a local radio host, while his father worked the family farm and was "a wallpaperer, plumber, painter or builder" rolled into one – "the original Mr Fixit," said Hayden. From his grandmother, who lived a few hundred yards away, came a lifelong interest in cooking. It was the great outdoors, however, that was his greatest love, and as well as cricket Hayden liked surfing, fishing and triathlons.

After school/university in Brisbane, Hayden graduated into the Queensland first XI, making his Sheffield Shield debut against South Australia at the Gabba in 1991. Beforehand, he'd innocently asked whether anyone had ever made a double-hundred on debut. Then, standing outside his crease and bashing the ball as if facing nothing more taxing than brother Gary's deliveries on the family farm, he threatened to do it, striking 149 from 229 balls with 23 fours. It was the first of three centuries in his opening four first-class games in a career that brought him 106 in all formats.

After regaining his Test place in 2000, Hayden – who hit 40 of those hundreds for Australia – embarked on a golden run that saw him become the world's No. 1-ranked batsman in Tests and one-day internationals by 2003. The catalyst was a tour to India in 2001, a poor one for Australia as they lost 2–1, ending a record sequence of 16 straight Test wins, but a personal triumph for Hayden, who top-scored with 549 runs in six innings. Starting with that series, Hayden scored 2,560 runs in 25 Tests with 11 hundreds. It prompted Steve Waugh, the Australia captain, to compare him to Don Bradman.

After winning seven of their next eight Test series, including two 4–1 triumphs over England, Waugh's side remained in their element when Zimbabwe visited for two Tests Down Under in 2003. As well as having recently retained the Ashes, Australia had won 3–1 in the West Indies earlier that year and gained a 2–0 victory at home to Bangladesh. Not even the fact that leading spinner Shane Warne was serving a 12-month drugs ban threatened further success against a Zimbabwe side making their maiden Test tour to Australia. In fact, Zimbabwe had won just seven of 67 games since entering Test cricket in 1992 and had lost nine in succession going into the series. Still Hayden was loath to take them for granted, approaching the task with tenacity typical of someone who, in his youth, had been rejected by the Australian Cricket Academy and its head coach, Rod Marsh, the former Australia wicketkeeper.

Prior to the series, Hayden had spent two months on North Stradbroke Island, about 19 miles south-east of Brisbane, and, as he put it, "trained my backside off". Day after strength-sapping day he ran up and down sand dunes until his legs felt like lead, insisting that he couldn't have been in better shape to produce a big innings. However, it was a world record that very nearly wasn't, for when Australia assembled for the First Test in Perth, Hayden injured his back in practice and admitted it was "line ball" whether he played. He did so only with the help of a vest to keep his back warm.

Proceedings at the WACA began sombrely. Before play, the sides observed 88 seconds' silence in memory of the 88 Australians who'd died in the Bali terrorist attack, the first anniversary of which fell during the match. The players wore black armbands and Peter Hughes, a Bali survivor, had spoken to the Australian team before the game at Steve Waugh's behest. "His parting message," said Hayden, "was 'make the most of every day'." On a morning so beautiful that man's inhumanity to man seemed only more poignant, Zimbabwe won the toss and chose to bowl. The sky was a dreamy shade of blue, although a brisk wind buffeted the sun-bleached stands and the grass banks beneath the WACA's six iconic floodlight towers. Hayden, his own black armband threatening to burst beneath the pressure of his bulging left bicep, strode out with opening partner Justin Langer before a small crowd that climbed to just 7,639, reflecting the weak nature of the opposition and the fact that Australia was preoccupied with the Rugby World Cup, which would start the next day. In fact, more people would watch the World Cup match between Namibia and Ireland at Sydney's Aussie Stadium than would attend the entire Second Test staged 100 yards away.

Langer and Hayden – the order in which they always appeared on the scorecard – first opened together at the end of the 2001 Ashes, sharing 158 in the final Test at the Oval. It was the first of five hundred stands in their first ten innings together, four of which exceeded 200. Hitherto, Hayden's opening partners in Tests were Michael Slater or Mark Taylor, but Taylor played the last of his 104 games in early 1999, and Slater the last of his 74 in the Fourth Test at Leeds in 2001. Langer, 11 months older than Hayden and about half a foot shorter, had also faced a battle to establish himself; after debuting in 1993, it was another five years before he became a regular feature. As deft and stylish as Hayden was brutal, the left-handed Langer started his career as a steady accumulator. But he turned himself into a glorious strokemaker, moving up from No. 3 to form with Hayden one of the greatest of all opening partnerships, the pair revolutionising the role by attacking with the verve of middle-order players. "We're all about really asserting ourselves," said Hayden. "We're about making sure the opposition feel how close we are... it starts with us."

Not only were Langer and Hayden batting partners, they were also best friends. The night before the Perth Test they shared a cigar on Langer's front lawn to mark the start of the international summer. "He started with a toast to absent friends, then we puffed on the cigar and looked at the stars," wrote Hayden. He added that the pair were united by a common work ethic but otherwise "diametrically opposed". For whereas Hayden faltered if he over-thought cricket, Langer flourished in "think-mode", his mantra that "the pain of discipline is nothing like the pain of disappointment" even hanging on his shower wall. Langer was a black belt in taekwondo but Hayden was the more forbidding of the pair. "We were the original good cop, bad cop," he said. "He'd be as smiling and happy as I was cold."

The old firm: Langer and Hayden, the best of friends and the best of openers.

Another factor bonded them – their Christian faith. This was evident in a simple gesture with which they marked the start of their partnership against Zimbabwe in Perth and, indeed, all their partnerships. "When we were playing together," wrote Hayden, "Alfie [Langer] and I developed a custom where he would mark centre as he faced the first ball of a Test, then I would cross it with a line when we changed strike to form the sign of the cross. When I was at the bowler's end while he was preparing to face the first ball I would mark centre and he would cross it when we changed ends. It was another anchor in our relationship. When we marked the sign of the cross at the crease I would always say a silent prayer: Whatever happens today is in your hands."

Against a limited Zimbabwe attack, with 29-year-old pace-bowling captain Heath Streak its only star, Langer and Hayden began ominously. They put on 43 in nine overs before Langer chopped on to Sean Ervine, a 20-year-old all-rounder playing his third Test. Hayden, batting within himself at first, hit straight and hard when a bad ball arrived. An early example came when Streak overpitched and Hayden, with classic high elbow and follow-through, bullied him to the mid-off boundary across an outfield as fast as the WACA pitch. At lunch, both Hayden and Ricky Ponting had 31, with Australia 93 for one from 28 overs. Streak's decision to bowl – hoping for early assistance that never materialised – already looked a serious misjudgement.

Ponting departed for 37, lbw to Ervine, but Hayden reached a 107-ball half-century with seven fours and a five. This came when he took a quick single to mid-off and Streak, in trying to run him out, sent the ball bouncing off the stumps for four overthrows. Hayden reached his half-century with a rare aggressive shot, dancing down the track to launch 27-year-old left-arm spinner Ray Price – nephew of the former world No. 1 golfer Nick Price – for four. At the other end, Damien Martyn, a 31-year-old right-hander, struck 53 before edging opening batsman Trevor Gripper's off-spin to slip. At tea, Hayden had 76 and Steve Waugh four out of 203 for three from 56 overs.

As his 15th Test century came into view, Hayden – winning his 45th cap – had a stroke of bad luck immediately followed by a slice of good fortune. First, he got a clear bottom-edge when sweeping Price to the boundary between wicketkeeper Tatenda Taibu's legs only for umpire Venkat to signal four byes. Then, he miscued Price fractionally over the cover field, "the perfect example of the nervous nineties," said Richie Benaud on the Channel Nine commentary. Hayden reached three figures with a sweep to long-leg off Gripper, having faced 210 balls and hit 13 fours in over five hours' batting. He then decided to go for the bowling, racing from 100 to 150 in just 32 deliveries. Streak was smashed for four down the ground – "magnificent clubbing," purred Channel Nine's Ian Healy, the former Australian wicketkeeper – and then positively slaughtered for a straight for six. Price and Gripper were similarly treated, Hayden having dispensed with his helmet in favour of his Baggy Green cap as if to emphasise the change of gear. Australia scored 169 in the final session in 34 overs to finish the day on 372 for three, 107 of those post-tea runs to Hayden, whose total stood at 183. "As long as Hayden maintains his desire," observed the writer Lynn McConnell, "the prospects for individual records are limitless."

In initially cloudy, breezy weather, Hayden and Waugh continued a stand worth 173 when day two began. Only 8,062 were there to see history made, part of an aggregate attendance of 24,051 across the five days. Thanks to his pre-series training on North Stradbroke Island, Hayden felt fresh and had now removed the vest for his back. "My concentration was still good and I was seeing and hitting the ball just as clearly," he said. Hayden further ascribed his freshness to a menu item at the team hotel. Each night he dined on smoked ham and pumpkin soup, describing it as "big enough for me to feel satisfied, small enough not to weigh me down". Hayden said that the time difference in Perth always threw out his body clock and upset his eating patterns. He called the soup "a perfect meal" and "a key part of that innings".

The next milestone in front of him was his double-hundred, which he reached after half an hour's play. His second century took 82 balls and he'd now hit 26 fours to go with three sixes. Waugh fell for 78, caught and bowled by

Ervine, after adding 207 with Hayden in 45 overs. Hayden then passed his Test-best of 203 against India at Chennai in 2001, followed by his first-class best of 235 not out for Hampshire against Warwickshire at Southampton in 1997. As his assault on the straight boundaries continued apace (Hayden's fifth half-century contained another four sixes), the Channel Nine commentators voiced admiration. "He goes downtown!" exclaimed Hayden's former opening partner and captain Mark Taylor, when Streak was clobbered back over his head. "He goes a long way downtown! In fact, it goes all the way! Well, that's a shot of nonchalant ease. It wasn't a bad delivery from Heath Streak... Matthew Hayden just hit through the line." When Gripper was insouciantly deposited over long-on, the former Australian captain Ian Chappell remarked that Hayden was "terrorising the spectators", a feat he twice repeated in quick succession as if for the benefit of anyone who'd missed it. "Sitting back in your armchairs," said Richie Benaud, his velvety tones conveying the equivalent of a raised eyebrow, "you might think this is a fairly small ground the way Hayden's treating it, but it's not... full-size job."

With no trace of sweat beneath wavy blond hair, Hayden now looked like a man having a net in the middle of a Test match. He hit the ball so hard – and with such apparent ease – that his shots resounded like artillery fire. He called again for his Baggy Green cap, as if to show that the pitch and bowling held no terrors, and proceeded like a one-man threshing machine. "He is absolutely murdering Zimbabwe," said Channel Nine's former England captain Tony Greig – or, as the former England coach David Lloyd might have put it, "He's flippin' murdering 'em."

Man-mountain in motion: Hayden hammers Zimbabwe in Perth.

There was now a feeling of "pity poor Zimbabwe", the sun emerging to add to their woes. The pitch and conditions gave them nothing; the sky was a mocking ceiling of blue. To their credit, however, they kept on trying and stubbornly refused to throw in the towel. Their bowlers charged in, their fielders walked in, and there was no suggestion of declining mood. Perhaps the mere act of leaving behind their troubled country was sufficient motivation. Zimbabwe had become a brutal police state under Robert Mugabe, a president who required no second invitation to politicise cricket for personal ends. Since the turn of the millennium, the Zimbabwe Cricket Union, under pressure from Mugabe's repugnant regime, had effectively run a quota system to fast-track blacks at whites' expense. Murray Goodwin, the former Zimbabwe batsman, had said so prior to the

Australian tour, arguing that the side was no longer being picked on merit. It was a side depleted by the retirements of batsman/wicketkeeper Andy Flower and fast bowler Henry Olonga, who'd made a brave black-armband protest against the "death of democracy" in Zimbabwe during the World Cup earlier that year. All-rounder Guy Whittall had also retired, while Flower's brother, Grant, another fine batsman, was unavailable due to a finger injury. Within months of the Australian tour, Streak would take a long list of his players' grievances to the board and be sacked for his pains. Most would staunchly go on strike in protest, plunging Zimbabwe cricket into further chaos.

Some 11 months prior to the Perth Test, Steve Waugh had made this statement: "I would not trade Matthew Hayden for anybody else in world cricket. If anyone is going to break Brian Lara's world record Test score of 375, he is the man."

As Zimbabwe toiled beneath sunwashed skies, the sense was starting to build that something special was now in the offing. Gripper had sensed it from day one, when the tourists first banged their heads against the high brick wall of Hayden's bat. "Once he got to 60 or 70 it looked pretty ominous," he said. "It was like he was batting with a barn door." Having lost Waugh in the day's ninth over, Hayden put on 96 in 14 overs with Darren Lehmann, a stocky 33-year-old left-hander who would have made more than 27 Test appearances but for the galaxy of talent in Australia at the time. Lehmann hit 30 from 48 balls before, like Waugh, popping back a return catch to Ervine. Adam Gilchrist, a 31-year-old who revolutionised the wicketkeeper's role by also transforming games with the bat, arrived to add 13 to a lunchtime score of 524 for five (Hayden 271). "By now, a curious calm had come over Hayden," wrote *Wisden*. "His concentration did not waver until after he had passed the revered Australian number of 334, set by Don Bradman and equalled by Mark Taylor."

Bradman's score in the 1930 Headingley Test, when he beat Andy Sandham's record, was matched by Taylor against Pakistan at Peshawar in 1998. Taylor declared after clipping the final ball of the second day's play off left-arm spinner Aamer Sohail to square leg, where Ijaz Ahmed threw down a hand to stop the single. The popular myth, which Taylor denied, was that he refused to continue in the morning out of respect for "The Don". In reality, Taylor felt that a total of 599 for four was more than sufficient and did not want anyone to think he was batting on for personal prestige. The game petered out as Pakistan replied with 580 for nine declared, Taylor striking 92 in the second innings before hands were shaken.

In 2012, a similar act of self-sacrifice was performed by another Australian captain, Michael Clarke, who declared when 329 not out against India in Sydney. "It's about putting the team first," said Clarke, whose triple inspired an innings victory inside four days. "I didn't think about it [records] at all," he added. "I didn't have Don Bradman or Mark Taylor's score in my head whatsoever."

It was fitting that Taylor was now at the microphone as Hayden climbed the ladder of history. A single off Streak saw him become only the second man to score a Test triple-hundred in Australia after the classical left-hander Bob Cowper, who made 307 against England at Melbourne in 1966. Hayden, whose third century came from 70 balls, celebrated by lofting Price for another straight maximum. Even his miscues were clearing the rope. "He's seeing the ball about water-melon size at the moment," said Taylor, who rose to his feet in the commentary box when Hayden passed 334 by driving Gripper to long-off for a single. No sooner had the collective applause subsided than Hayden offered his solitary chance, skying Ervine to long-on where Mark Vermeulen shelled a sitter. "It's out!... Oh dear!" sighed an incredulous Benaud as the catch went down, his voice a mixture of revulsion and relief. Then, as the incongruously incautious nature of the shot sank in, Benaud, in total disbelief, said, "Well, from that, can we conclude that he [Hayden] either doesn't know, or no one's told him about, the Brian Lara 375?"

As it turned out, Hayden was fully aware of it thanks to batting partner Gilchrist, his "milestone mentor". Hayden wrote: "We'd hear the crowd clap and I'd ask Gilly, 'What was that for?' He'd say, 'Well, you've just passed Bob Simpson [311] and Sir Garfield Sobers [365] is coming up, but you have Wally Hammond and Len Hutton and the boys to contend with at the moment.'" Once he beat Bradman and Taylor's 334, Hayden thought he might as well "have a crack" at the record but said he felt increasingly self-conscious. "Suddenly, the show had become all about me rather than the result of the game, and that's not the way cricket's supposed to be." Hayden claimed he'd secretly wanted Waugh to declare, adding: "When you're used to playing as part of a team, sure, there are great personal moments, but when the whole shooting match revolves around you – 21 other players, the officials and all the spectators just waiting for you to get something done, you do feel pretty exposed." Hayden now passed the highest Test score since Lara – Sanath Jayasuriya's 340 for Sri Lanka against India at Colombo in

1997. Going into the final day of a game going nowhere, with Sri Lanka 587 for one in reply to India's 537 for eight declared, Jayasuriya, a dashing left-handed opener, was 326 with the record at his mercy. More than 30,000 turned up only for Jayasuriya to be surprised by a ball of extra bounce from off-spinner Rajesh Chauhan, which he popped up to silly point. "I felt a great pressure on me when I came out to bat and obviously I am disappointed, but at least my country has made a great achievement," said Jayasuriya, with Sri Lanka's final total of 952 for six declared beating the previous highest Test score of 903 for seven declared by England against Australia at The Oval in 1938, when Hutton made his 364.

After reaching his 350 from 402 balls with 35 fours and ten sixes, Hayden sailed past Hutton and Sobers and closed in fast on Lara's mark. In the final over before tea, with his score on 373, he pulled Price for two to tie the record, receiving preliminary acclaim from the WACA crowd. Hayden played Price's next ball to mid-on for no run, then drove his next delivery to long-on for a single to enter territory never explored.

As soon as he hit the historic shot, which sparked great scenes around the ground, Hayden threw both hands aloft. He twirled his bat in his right arm three times as he jogged down to complete the run, then broke out into an expansive grin. He removed and kissed his Baggy Green cap, acknowledged the cheering crowd and embraced Gilchrist. The rest of the Australian team stood applauding on the balcony – fast bowler Jason Gillespie high-fiving colleagues – and the players all came down to congratulate him as he walked off at tea, having scored 105 runs during the session.

Hayden added one more boundary after the break then fell to the third ball of the session for 380, sweeping Gripper

Hayden acknowledges the crowd after passing Lara's 375

to deep backward square where Stuart Carlisle took an excellent, tumbling catch. "My first thought," said Hayden, "was, 'thank God that's over'." Waugh declared immediately, Australia's 735 for six their second-highest Test total and highest at home. Gilchrist finished with 113 from 94 balls after adding with Hayden 233 in 34 overs. Gilchrist had gone to his hundred from 84 balls, his own outstanding performance reduced to a footnote. Hayden batted for ten hours, 22 minutes (around two and a half hours less than Lara) and faced 437 balls (101 fewer than Lara). He hit 38 fours and his total of 11 sixes was second to Wasim Akram's Test record of 12 for Pakistan against Zimbabwe at Sheikhupura in 1996. All five Zimbabwe bowlers conceded over 100 runs, Price the most expensive with nought for 187 from 36 overs. Left with three days and a session to survive,

Zimbabwe were dismissed for 239 and 321 to lose by an innings and 175 runs. They lost the Second Test at Sydney by nine wickets, Hayden adding scores of 20 and 101 not out to finish with 501 – Lara's number – for the series.

Although Hayden admitted that Zimbabwe were "one of the weaker Test outfits I faced", he said of his record in Perth: "I don't think I ever hit the ball better in Test cricket than I did in that innings." However, newspapers were quick to put the performance into context. Peter Roebuck, the former Somerset captain, wrote in the *Sydney Morning Herald*: "Through the glory of the moment, though, comes a nagging sense of unease. What does it all mean? Of course, the notion that Bradman and the rest scored their runs against tight and fresh attacks operating on helpful pitches is false. Nonetheless, there was always a feeling the teams belonged on the same field. Unfortunately, the same cannot be said of the teams appearing in Perth. Test cricket has compromised its most precious asset – its legitimacy." Roebuck added: "Although it was hardly Hayden's fault, this was not so much a contest as a demolition. Among the Zimbabweans only the captain has earned his stripes as a Test player. Hayden was not wrenching runs from a reluctant opponent. He was taking sweets from a child. Test status has been spread around in an attempt to widen the game and to secure votes on the governing body." Nonetheless, as Robert Craddock observed in the *Daily Telegraph*, "Modern cricket has become overloaded with numbing statistics but this is truly special and quite appropriate that arguably the greatest side in cricket history now has a milestone that will stand as eternal testament to the cavalier way they play the game. The farmer's son from Kingaroy, who still finishes most of his

All for one, one for all: Hayden celebrates with his Australian team-mates.

sentences with 'Eh?' has gone where none of the 2,367 men
to play the game have gone."

No one appreciated the "truly special" nature of the feat
more than Lara, who telephoned Hayden from Jamaica.
According to Hayden, the West Indian said: "Well done,
great things happen to good cricketers. You and your team
deserve it." Hayden said it was "fantastic to hear his words"
and described Lara as his "favourite player by a street".
However, he admitted that he "always sensed that Lara
hated me", in so doing referencing the ultimate paradox of
his own story: namely, that he was, as the former England
seam bowler Angus Fraser wrote, "one of the nastiest
sledgers Australia has produced", a man who could be "a pig
to play against" and who, from the slips or gully, would say

"horribly insulting things to batsmen". Although hardly alone in that, and, as Fraser qualified, "having a beer at the close of play he would be charming", Hayden was a Jekyll and Hyde character: on the one hand, a devout Christian who described his faith as "everything to me"; on the other, an aggressor hell-bent on gaining a psychological advantage, a man whose attitude seemed to be "love thy neighbour" – unless you happened to be playing cricket against him. It was a paradox that Hayden recognised and justified by defining Christianity as "who I am" and intimidating opponents as "a role I played". Some thought it a rather convenient distinction, not to say fundamentally hypocritical. "My role became one of intimidator," he wrote. "And, just as a good actor completely gives himself to a part, I went all the way. Apart from an incident where I kicked a dressing-room door, I didn't break the rules of the game, but I played at a time when the spirit of the game was changing, becoming more professional, psychological and physical, when teams were learning to use whatever arsenal they could find as well as the bat and the ball. I might not always have been proud of my actions, and I wasn't always popular for them, but I recognised the importance of that part of my role, which helped my team become one of the most dominant of all time... Was I a hypocrite? Maybe. But I am what I am: a man of contradictions." Hayden cited the example of Saint Peter, who, for all his "foibles and flaws", came to be known as "the rock of the church". "For all my shortcomings," he added, "I wanted to be one of the rocks of the Australian cricket team."

Hayden, who felt that "the hype around sledging was overblown", came to epitomise the term "mental disintegration", the leitmotif of Steve Waugh's strategy. Allan

Border was credited with initiating a concept that recognised top-level sport is played as much in the mind. Hayden said that Australia created "an aura of intensity that no other side could match" and that teams "lost the battle for mental supremacy sometimes before the match had started". Hayden noted that "we weren't playing tiddlywinks" but added, somewhat sadly perhaps, that he "deliberately avoided getting to know Lara or [Sachin] Tendulkar on a personal level" as he "couldn't afford to fraternise with them" since they were "a threat". He thought that dropping his guard could expose vulnerability, saying: "We'd find it hard to think of someone as a great bloke and then go out and try to destroy their self-esteem." "Even so," he said, "it killed me to distance myself from Lara in particular, but I learned so much simply by watching him play."

Hayden's respect for Lara the batsman was unequivocal. "Brian Lara just captivated me. Every time he took to the crease it was like a batting tutorial... He was ruthless, calculating and brutally effective. I hated it and loved it at the same time." Records, though, were never Hayden's goal, statistics purely incidental to him. There were enough of those to fill a chapter, another two that stand out being his average opening partnership in Test cricket with Langer (51.88) and with Gilchrist in one-day internationals (48.39). Perhaps Hayden's attitude was best summed up by this remark after taking down Lara's 375, one that stands as a tribute to him.

"I'm just thrilled that I was wearing the Baggy Green cap when the record was broken," said a man who embodied its selfless values.

Australia v Zimbabwe

Played at W. A. C. A. Ground, Perth, on 9, 10, 11, 12, 13 October, 2003.

Toss: Zimbabwe. Result: Australia won by an innings and 175 runs.

AUSTRALIA

J. L. Langer b Ervine 26	†A. C. Gilchrist not out. 113
M. L. Hayden c Carlisle b Gripper 380	B 4, lb 10, w 1, nb 3 18
R. T. Ponting lbw b Ervine 37	
D. R. Martyn c Wishart b Gripper 53	1/43 (1) (6 wkts dec, 146.3 overs) 735
*S. R. Waugh c and b Ervine 78	2/102 (3) 3/199 (4)
D. S. Lehmann c and b Ervine 30	4/406 (5) 5/502 (6) 6/735 (2)

A. J. Bichel, B. Lee, J. N. Gillespie and S. C. G. MacGill did not bat.

Streak 26–6–131–0; Blignaut 28–4–115–0; Ervine 31–4–146–4; Price 36–5–187–0;
Gripper 25.3–0–142–2.

ZIMBABWE

D. D. Ebrahim b Gillespie 29	–	b Gillespie	4
T. R. Gripper c Lehmann b Lee 53	–	c Gilchrist b Gillespie	0
M. A. Vermeulen c Hayden b MacGill. 38	–	c Gilchrist b Lee	63
S. V. Carlisle c Hayden b MacGill 2	–	c Hayden b Lehmann	35
C. B. Wishart c Gilchrist b Bichel 46	–	lbw b Bichel	8
C. N. Evans b Bichel 22	–	b Lehmann	5
†T. Taibu lbw b Gillespie 15	–	c Gilchrist b Bichel	3
*H. H. Streak b Lee 9	–	(9) not out	71
S. M. Ervine c Waugh b Gillespie 6	–	(8) b Bichel	53
A. M. Blignaut lbw b Lee 0	–	st Gilchrist b Lehmann	22
R. W. Price not out 2	–	c Waugh b Bichel	36
Lb 10, w 2, nb 5 17		B 4, lb 6, w 5, nb 6	21

1/61 (1) 2/105 (2) 3/120 (4)   (89.3 overs) 239   1/2 (2) 2/11 (1)   (127.2 overs) 321
4/131 (3) 5/199 (5) 6/200 (6)   3/110 (3) 4/112 (4)
7/231 (7) 8/231 (8) 9/231 (10) 10/239 (9)   5/118 (5) 6/126 (7) 7/126 (6)
                                                      8/209 (8) 9/247 (10) 10/321 (11)

Lee 15–4–48–3; Gillespie 25.3–9–52–3; Bichel 21–2–62–2; MacGill 21–4–54–2;
Lehmann 2–1–3–0; Waugh 5–1–10–0. *Second innings*—Lee 35–8–96–1; Gillespie 3–0–6–2;
MacGill 3.4–1–10–0; Bichel 28.2–15–63–4; Lehmann 31.2–15–61–3; Martyn 13–5–34–0;
Waugh 8–2–26–0; Ponting 5–1–15–0.

Umpires: S. Venkataraghavan and P. Willey.   Third umpire: S. J. Davis.

Referee: G. R. Viswanath.

11

Brian Lara (400*)
West Indies versus England
Antigua 2004

"To break the most famous of all batting records once might conceivably be ascribed to good fortune. To do it twice is proof of pure genius."

So proclaimed *The Times* after Brian Lara reclaimed his world record just 185 days after Matthew Hayden had snatched it from him. Remarkably, Lara did so at the same ground where he scored the 375, against the same opponents, in the same month, on the same day of the week and at almost exactly the same time of day. The similarities were striking, the symmetry sweet.

For all the guts and glory of Hayden's 380, there was a sense, particularly in the West Indies, that he'd pinched the record under false pretences. After all, Zimbabwe were no England, a major Test-playing nation, their bowling no better than county standard. As such, there was a feeling that a record that belonged to West Indies for 45 years through Lara and Garry Sobers had never quite left its spiritual home and was only on loan to Hayden at best. As Gus Logie, the West Indies coach, said: "Brian was one of the first people to congratulate Matthew Hayden, but I think deep down he felt that the record was his."

Lara claimed that he was happy that Hayden took the record – "the bane of my existence for quite some time". He said that he was "relieved" and able to "move on" and that he'd swap any records for a winning West Indies. "It was not a sad moment at all," he said – adding, with reference to his first-class record 501, that the "double world record-holder [tag] followed me". Lara maintained that "it was never my focus to preserve the records or not have anybody break the records or, if they did, be upset about it". Even so, it would take an unusually magnanimous man to have held that belief privately.

The Lara who regained the world record was a different Lara to the one who'd seized it. In 1994 he was a fresh-faced 24-year-old who savoured the simple enjoyment of batting. But once he pulled the ball from Chris Lewis that took him past Sobers's 365 and then, 49 days later, cover-drove John Morris to go past Hanif Mohammad's 499, his life changed. Innocence evaporated amid fame, riches and instant celebrity and the media frenzy that swallowed him up. Within a year, Lara would say that "cricket is ruining my life" as fears developed for his mental state. He temporarily walked out of the 1995 tour of England after a row with his captain, Richie Richardson, and refused to go on the subsequent trip to Australia. Worn down by fatigue and the endless focus on him, there was even talk of him quitting the sport. As Nasser Hussain, the former England captain, wrote: "There is no doubt that Brian changed after that innings [375] and his 501 for Warwickshire a few weeks later. He became more wary. He didn't know who he could trust and who his real friends were any more… I suppose in that knock in Antigua he went from mere mortal to the greatest batsman in the world, and it was bound to have an effect on him."

To compound matters, West Indies were now in sharp decline, a shadow of the side that Lara entered. In early 1995 they'd lost 2–1 at home to Australia, a result that marked the transfer of power from one team to the other. It was West Indies' first Test series defeat for 15 years and 29 series: the first of 14 defeats, in fact, in 27 series prior to England's arrival in 2004. By then, fast-bowling spearheads Courtney Walsh and Curtly Ambrose had followed Viv Richards, Malcolm Marshall, Jeffrey Dujon and Gordon Greenidge into retirement and there were no obvious replacements from a domestic system badly administered and poorly funded. As the brightest star in a waning firmament, Lara had plenty on his plate. In addition, his critics accused him of selfishness and of putting his interests first. Some said that he undermined Walsh to get the West Indies captaincy in 1998 and that his ego was bigger than his towering scores. Throughout his career, Lara was praised and pilloried with gusto.

By the time that England landed in 2004, he was in his second spell as West Indies captain, the first having finished four years earlier with nine defeats in 11 Tests. He returned to the role after the 2003 World Cup and immediately suffered a bruising defeat at home to Australia. They won the first three Tests before West Indies won the fourth and final match in Antigua by three wickets with a Test-record chase of 418, thereby avoiding their first home whitewash and giving Lara his "greatest cricketing experience". Optimism quickly vanished, however, with West Indies in the midst of a terrible run of ten defeats in 14 Tests that left only Zimbabwe and Bangladesh below them in the world rankings and Lara's position again under threat. Discontent intensified when England also went 3–0 up in the four-match series in 2004, which, for them, was a stepping-stone towards their ultimate aim of regaining the Ashes the following year. Backed by some 10,000 travelling fans in islands where they'd not won a Test series for 36 years, England triumphed on what *Wisden* called "unexpectedly helpful pitches" that were "a reaction to the bland surfaces on which Australia had built huge totals the previous year". Those pitches played into the hands of England's four-pronged pace attack, which performed a key role when England indeed won the Ashes in 2005 – six years after they'd plunged to the bottom of the rankings before Hussain and coach Duncan Fletcher dragged them up by their bootstraps. Now England and West Indies were on opposite trajectories, and where once it was the Caribbean quick bowlers who threatened life and limb, now England captain Michael Vaughan held the aces in the form of Steve Harmison, Matthew Hoggard, Andrew Flintoff and Simon Jones, a quartet that played just 16 Tests together but left an indelible mark in that time.

Vaughan's chief threat in the Caribbean was Harmison, the 25-year-old Durham man who came of age during this series. Tall and gangly with the ability to generate steep bounce à la Ambrose, Harmison had shown only flashes of promise since his debut around 18 months earlier. He'd struggled with injuries and flown home from a recent tour of Bangladesh with a back problem amid accusations of a diffident attitude. But time on the comeback trail spent training with his beloved Newcastle United Football Club – in particular, observing the fierce work ethic of striker Alan Shearer – inspired Harmison to new levels of fitness and determination and Vaughan to contend that he was on the cusp of "something special".

Quite how special was seen during the First Test in Jamaica which England won by ten wickets after Harmison's seven for 12 routed the West Indies for 47 in their second innings, their lowest Test total. At one stage, Vaughan had eight slips and a short leg because "I couldn't see the ball going anywhere else". He described it as "some of the most devastating fast bowling ever witnessed" and "one of the greatest spells by an England bowler". The *Daily Mirror* christened the hero of the hour "Grievous Bodily Harmison", a nickname almost as good as his spell.

Prior to the Second Test in Trinidad, the England players were invited to the house that Lara built on the land given him by the government for his 375. Overlooking Port-of-Spain's vast Savannah, the hilltop retreat was the type of luxurious mansion that a pop star might own, highlighting Lara's rise from humble beginnings. Vaughan described the experience as "a fascinating diversion" and said that "the house reminded me of a kind of American bachelor pad with

Brian Lara's house in the hills overlooking Port-of-Spain. The England players visited prior to the second Test in Trinidad.

every gadget and mod con imaginable". Not that England repaid Lara's generosity; they dismissed him for nought and eight at Queen's Park Oval having dismissed him for 23 and nought in Jamaica. Harmison got him both times in Trinidad, where England won by seven wickets after Harmison's first innings six-wicket haul was followed by Jones's maiden Test five-for. Jones, 25, of Glamorgan, returned to Test cricket in this series after a terrible injury at Brisbane in 2002, when he ruptured a cruciate knee ligament in trying to stop a boundary. England's victory in Trinidad was immediately followed by the resignation of West Indies' manager Ricky Skerritt, who lamented his inability "to instill in the entire team the fullest understanding of their obligations on and off the field to the people of the West Indies". Skerritt was referring in no small part to events that followed the opening Test, when several of his players partied in the ground with West Indian fans directly after the match had been lost. *Wisden* wrote of players "dancing giddily in the stands, partying with their supporters as though ten-wicket defeats by England were all in a day's work".

Two-nil up with two Tests to play, thereby retaining the Wisden Trophy recovered in 2000 after 27 years of West Indian ownership, England sealed the series outright with a three-day win in Barbados. This time it was Flintoff, the 26-year-old Lancashire all-rounder, who claimed his maiden Test five-for, including Lara for 36 as West Indies scored 224 in their first innings. An unbeaten 119 from Graham Thorpe, the 34-year-old Surrey left-hander, secured a two-run lead before Hoggard, the 27-year-old Yorkshireman, tilted a well-balanced game with England's tenth Test hat-trick, dismissing Ramnaresh Sarwan, Shivnarine Chanderpaul and Ryan Hinds. West Indies were shot out for 94, Lara top-scoring with 33 before England knocked off a 93-run target for the loss of two wickets to spark a party to which no one objected.

By now, the vultures were not so much circling at Lara's door as greedily devouring its hinges, his team stumbling from one disaster to the next. Having narrowly avoided a first home whitewash the previous year, that spectre loomed again amid suggestions of dressing-room disharmony. As Lara conceded ahead of the final Test in Antigua: "The next five days are very important in terms of my future as captain. No captain, no team wants to go down for the first time in their history as losing all their Test matches at home."

It didn't take long for England's party mood to vanish. They arrived in Antigua to find that they were staying at the same hotel as many of their supporters who, said Vaughan, "wanted to sing when we wanted to sleep". Members of the Barmy Army, the England fans' group, knocked on players' doors hoping for an autograph and possibly a chat. While fully appreciative of their noisy backing, which had given the Barbados Test, in particular, the feel of a home game, Vaughan felt "we should not have been in that kind of environment". Furthermore, he said that practice facilities at the Recreation Ground were "far from ideal" and there were "ructions in the camp" because of it. The pitch for the Test, overseen by the former West Indies fast bowler Andy Roberts, seemed specifically designed to counter a whitewash. "A pancake could not have been flatter had a ten-ton steamroller gone over it a thousand times," lamented Vaughan, thereby evoking gloriously improbable imagery. *Wisden* said that the pitch "would have lasted for all of the 12 days that it had taken to decide the other three Tests".

Lara won the toss and, for the fourth successive time in the series, West Indies batted first. They recalled Ricardo Powell, a hard-hitting 25-year-old more than four years after his solitary cap, Chanderpaul making way after scoring 101 runs in six innings at 16.83 (Lara's return was fractionally worse: 100 runs in six innings at 16.66). England showed two changes. Ashley Giles, the 31-year-old left-arm spinner, had a stomach bug and was replaced by Gareth Batty, the 26-year-old Worcestershire off-spinner. More significantly, England replaced the 25-year-old Nottinghamshire wicket-keeper Chris Read with Kent debutant Geraint Jones, 27, a decision that caused appreciable controversy. Although Read's glovework had been impeccable, his highest score in 11 Tests was 38 not out. Vaughan admitted the decision was "a bit harsh" but said England wanted to look at Jones with the series won and that he had the capacity to make hundreds from No. 7. However, as Mike Walters put it in the *Daily Mirror*, "it would have taken Indiana Jones to stop Lara".

The great man strode to the crease beneath clear blue skies after Flintoff trapped Daren Ganga lbw in the 14th over. England thought they had Lara caught behind fourth ball for a duck but Australian umpire Darrell Hair ruled there was no thin edge to a drive at Harmison (TV replays suggested he was right). Along with Thorpe, Hair was the only other man on the field throughout both of Lara's Test record innings. However, Hussain appeared briefly as a substitute fielder in 1994 and now, along with Thorpe and Mark Butcher, formed the experienced nucleus of England's

Steve Harmison, third from left, is convinced that he's had Brian Lara caught behind for a duck only for umpire Darrell Hair to disagree. Wicketkeeper Geraint Jones, Graham Thorpe and Mark Butcher look similarly nonplussed.

batting, *Wisden* observing that "the series would not have been won by England had it not been for the bravery and professional know-how of the three thirty-somethings in the middle order".

Following his close shave on nought, Vaughan said that Lara "never looked like getting out" and that the only thing capable of doing it was "a missile". But he struggled for fluency early on and was troubled by his right little finger, which he'd dislocated when dropping a slip catch during the first Test. Although it didn't keep him out of the subsequent Tests, Lara missed the first of seven one-day internationals the week after the Antigua match to allow the problem to settle. The one-day series ended 2–2 after two of the fixtures were abandoned and the other washed out.

On an Antigua pitch that mocked the bowlers, Lara followed his early play-and-miss at Harmison by striking his next delivery for four, squirting him behind backward point to open his account. Jones was lightly leg-glanced to the rope as Lara reached 17 at lunch, which West Indies took at 98 for two after losing Chris Gayle to the penultimate ball of the session, the opener patting back a return to Batty after scoring 69 from 80 deliveries. During the interval, the weather worsened and rain washed out the afternoon session. When play resumed in bright sunshine, with a brisk wind blowing the English flags that pledged allegiance to practically every Premiership and Football League club, West Indies dominated the pleasant evening. Lara reached a 61-ball half-century with seven boundaries, four of them off Hoggard, whom he three times cut with princely flourish. He ended the day on 86 out of 208 for two, with Sarwan unbeaten on 41, the third-wicket pair having shared 110 at just over four runs an over. With Lara back to his sparkling best, Vaughan was already fearing the worst. "I was already thinking Matthew Hayden's world record 380 would not last," he said.

Sunshine and streaky white clouds greeted the players on day two, which Lara opened by driving its first ball, from Hoggard, to the off-side fence. It was the shot of a man who looked as if he'd already been batting for hours that morning, and was followed by a sumptuous whipped boundary off Hoggard through midwicket. "That's the shot of a fantastic player," said Tony Cozier, the voice of West Indies cricket, on Sky television. Co-commentator David Lloyd agreed. "Doesn't get any better than this… Just look at how he manoeuvres the ball." With cuts and pulls and flashing drives, fashioned from the usual trademark high back-lift, Lara's wristwork was sublime, as if he was playing table tennis at times. The crowd loved it, even though most of the 10,000 present were England supporters. "The Rec" erupted when Lara reached his 25th Test century – and seventh against England – by cutting Hoggard for another boundary, his 13th from 131 balls faced. Hussain, fielding at short leg, recalled: "He just looked at me when he got to about 100 as if to say, 'I might go after my record here.' He knew that it was such a flat pitch."

For one brief moment, England thought they'd dashed such hopes. When Lara had 127, he ran Jones down to third man and charged back for a second run as Hoggard threw in a fine return. The ball hit the stumps on the bounce and Aleem Dar, the square-leg umpire, sent the matter upstairs. Direct hits are often much closer than they look but replays showed that Lara had just got home. Hoggard was in the thick of it again when Lara pushed Vaughan's off-spin into the off side and set off running. This time, Hoggard's throw missed and flew for four overthrows, giving Lara five runs. He reached his 150 as lunch approached, from 199 balls with 18 fours, but lost Sarwan on the stroke of it. Caught in two minds whether to play or leave Harmison, his 23-year-old partner edged to first slip, having scored 90 and shared with him 232 in 58 overs. Lara lunched on 165 out of 342 for three, with Ricardo Powell unbeaten on four.

Already without the stricken Giles, England lost Hoggard to similar symptoms, forcing Vaughan to bowl Batty more than he wished. The Yorkshire-born Batty – blond, feisty, and infectiously competitive – gave everything, but it would have needed Nora Batty to shoo Lara from the middle,

Take that: Lara launches Gareth Batty for six as Andrew Flintoff looks on at slip.

Vaughan conceding that "we could have included McGrath and Murali and it wouldn't have made a difference". After Powell departed to a top-edged hook, ending "an innings every bit as awful as Lara's was awesome", thought the *Daily Telegraph*, Lara struck his first six when Batty was launched back over his head. "He's hit it beautifully," said the former England captain David Gower on commentary. "Perfect follow-through. That's almost Sobers-like, that follow-through." A swept boundary off Batty took Lara to 199 and then a leg-side single off the same bowler raised his 200. Lara punched the air but, when he removed his helmet, there was no trace of a smile – only something more resembling annoyance after his paltry pickings earlier in the series. "One has the feeling there's still plenty of petrol left in the tank," said Gower, once Lara had reached his latest milestone from 260 balls with 22 fours to go with the six. As it turned out, the tank was exactly half-full.

Lara launched Batty for another straight six and, at tea, had 224 out of 449 for four. He'd now gone past his third-highest Test score of 221, against Sri Lanka at Colombo in 2001, behind only the 375 against England in 1994 and the 277 against Australia at Sydney the previous year. Lara's 688 runs in that 2001 Sri Lanka series was second only to Graham Gooch's 752 for England against India in 1990 as the most achieved in a three-match rubber. Lara got the better of Muttiah Muralitharan, the great Sri Lanka off-spinner, just as he got the better of Shane Warne, the great Australia leg-spinner, during his other standout series in 1999. Then, as in 2004, Lara was under intense pressure as captain on the back of a 5–0 whitewash in South Africa and a 312-run defeat to Australia in the First Test in Trinidad, where his side were bowled out for 51, then West Indies' lowest Test total. But Lara utterly transformed the series, scoring 213 in the Second Test in Jamaica – the innings he always rated as his best – as West Indies won by ten wickets. He followed that with an unbeaten 153 which inspired an incredible one-wicket victory in Barbados, putting the hosts 2–1 up. Australia won the final Test in Antigua by 176 runs, but not before Lara had cracked an 82-ball hundred.

At Antigua in 2004, Lara had added four to his score after tea when he suddenly played and missed at Harmison. "Well, he can afford one mistake – 228 on the board," quipped David Lloyd. Ryan Hinds, a 23-year-old left-hander, gave Batty his second return catch after adding 89 with Lara, who reached his 250 from 323 deliveries. In the jubilant stands, where the conch shells blared and the sound systems thumped, the chant went up: "No whitewash! No whitewash!"

Lara had a nervy moment on 292, sweeping Batty straight up only for the ball to land agonisingly behind wicketkeeper Jones, and an even nervier one on 293, when he gave his only chance – a half-chance really – when he crashed one back at Batty that burst through his hands and flew to the boundary. An off-side single off Batty then saw Lara become only the second man after Don Bradman to score two Test triple-hundreds, this one reached from 404 balls with 34 fours and two sixes. He celebrated with another punch of the air and something more akin to a smile, if not quite the full-blown beam that might have been warranted. At stumps, Lara had 313 out of 595 for five, with wicketkeeper Ridley Jacobs – a strong 36-year-old left-hander – unbeaten on 47.

Ten years earlier, Lara had endured a restless night on 320 as he contemplated Sobers's record. Ten years on, he found himself tossing and turning again, even phoning friends in England as he couldn't sleep. Lara had given himself time and licence to break the record, insisting that West Indies wanted 700-750 before declaring. A sunny third day was moments old when he hoisted their 600, turning opening batsman Marcus Trescothick's gentle medium-pace to the fine-leg boundary. From then on, it was a watchful procession to his 350, his seventh half-century the slowest of his innings, taking 90 balls and one hour, 42 minutes.

England's problems, already extensive, multiplied when Lara had 359. Harmison, the only man to have caused him much bother, received a third warning for running on the pitch and was forced out of the attack. "He didn't look overly concerned," quipped one writer, while Flintoff kept reminding his colleague that he was bowling his overs as well as his own. "But everything I tried on behalf of both of us," said Flintoff, "Lara seemed to have an answer for."

For the second time in his career, Lara went past Sobers's 365, as if to prove that the first occasion wasn't a fluke. He then brought up West Indies' 700 with a four to long-on off Vaughan, which lifted his score to 372. By now, the England captain admitted that he and his players "were actually willing him to do it [break the record]", adding that "the sheer majesty of it all had been a marvel to witness". Two more singles off Vaughan took Lara to 374 and then the record was equalled in audacious fashion. Betraying no sign of nerves, Lara charged Batty and hit him back over his head into the Sir Vivian Richards Pavilion for six, quietly punching the air as the fielders applauded. With one more needed to go past Hayden, the crowd left stunned by that fearless stroke, Vaughan brought his field in to cut off singles, the equivalent of trying to plug a burst dam by repositioning a handful of sandbags. Nothing had stopped the flow of runs, and nothing would stop the scenes that followed. Lara swept Batty's next ball past Thorpe to the fine-leg boundary to climb Mount Everest for a second time.

> "And there it is!" said Ian Bishop, the former West Indies fast bowler on commentary. "The world record has fallen once again to Brian Charles Lara of Trinidad and Tobago and the West Indies, the second time in his career that he's broken this record, and what a moment of history this is, a repeat performance. Ten years ago he set it, and he's done it again at the very ground."

No sooner had the ball gone past Thorpe, who bent down stiffly like a pensioner trying to apprehend a wind-blown hat, than Lara leapt twice in celebration as he ran towards the non-striker's end. His face was creased in utter joy, elation framed in every feature. He continued running almost halfway to the boundary before slowing down, turning and raising his hands to the crowd. He jogged all the way back to the non-striker's end and locked into a long embrace with Jacobs, his batting partner, before being congratulated in turn by the England players. "We were all happy for him," wrote Flintoff. "Lara was popular with the England lads and I went up and shook his hand after he broke the record and told him I was pleased for him and I meant that."

There was no pitch invasion as in 1994, or sight of Sobers striding out to bestow his blessing, but there was what *Wisden* termed "an inappropriate appearance by a

A popular assassin: the England players congratulate Lara.

government entourage headed by the new prime minister of Antigua and Barbuda, Baldwin Spencer". Apparently keen to share the limelight, like a photobomber who ruins pictures, Spencer – a well-built man in a navy jacket – hugged Lara and shook his hand, as did fellow ciphers while camera crews loitered. Once released from their self-absorbed grip, Lara embarked on a prolonged salute of the crowd, dancing and waving their flags in the background. The applause lasted for several minutes, Lara bending down to kiss the pitch just as he'd done a decade before. Finally, there was one last congratulatory pat from wicketkeeper Jones before Lara carefully replaced his helmet, took fresh guard and settled into his stance once more, meeting Batty's next ball with a textbook forward-defensive shot that said: "Thanks very much, everyone, but I haven't finished yet. I'd quite like 400 before I go." Sure enough, after Jacobs reached his third Test hundred on the stroke of lunch, which West Indies took at 734 for five (Lara 390), he stressed as much to David

Sealed with a kiss: Lara kisses the pitch on which he regained the world record.

Gower. Waiting with microphone beside the boundary, after Lara had walked through a tunnel of bats held up by team-mates, Gower – putting on his best rhetorical question face – said: "Sorry to have to ask you this, are you carrying on?" Lara smiled and replied somewhat sheepishly, "Yeah, we're carrying on. We need to get 750."

Lara hit Batty for another straight four just after lunch and inched towards the cherished 400. A single to third man off Flintoff took him to 399 and gave him strike for Batty's next over. Bob Willis, the former England captain, took up commentary:

> "Batty to Lara… There goes the sweep! There it is! Perhaps the most significant single ever in the history of Test match cricket. Brian Charles Lara becomes the first man in the history of the game to register a score of 400… 582 deliveries… 776 minutes with 43 fours and four sixes… A remarkable human being."

There was no leap of joy this time as Lara completed the historic run. Off came the helmet and out came a smile, a quiet one of "mission accomplished". Lara declared at the end of the over, half an hour into the afternoon session. West Indies' 751 for five was their second-highest Test score and the highest conceded by England. Jacobs finished with 107, having shared with Lara 282, a West Indies' sixth-wicket record.

Lara's was the tenth quadruple-hundred in first-class cricket and he was the second man to have twice reached that mark after Bill Ponsford, the Australian batsman of the inter-war period. *Wisden* said that Lara was "so composed, so concentrated, so invincible that he surely could have carried on to 500, or 600 if he had been so minded". As it was, some felt that he batted on too long anyway in terms of the overall objective – that of trying to win the game. Vaughan, despite marvelling at his efforts, said that Lara did England "a favour" because, "if he'd wanted to win the match, he would have declared long before he did". However, West Indies' coach Gus Logie said that it was a collective decision to continue batting and that it might have been different had the series still been alive.

Some of the strongest criticism came from Hayden's captain, Ricky Ponting, who said that West Indies' "whole first innings might have been geared around one individual performance" and "that's not the way the Australian team plays". Tony Greig, the former England captain, was even more scathing. "I'm certainly not raving about the innings," he said. "I have to praise it for the sheer fact that he stayed in for so long but it wasn't an innings that you could be in awe of. It was clear he had the record in mind and was just going to keep grinding it out until he got there. As far as I'm concerned that is not a good way to play the game, especially when you're the captain. It shows that Brian Lara is not a very good captain." Most, however, recognised the context of Lara's performance: a dead rubber, a captain under immense pressure – anxious, first and foremost, to prevent a whitewash – and the fact that the regaining of the world record brought considerable pride not only to him but also the Caribbean people.

There were still 240 overs left when Lara declared, time enough, possibly, to force what was only an outside chance of a result. Ironically, had Lara not dropped Flintoff at slip off Sarwan just before stumps on day three, West Indies might have caused more tremors after reducing England to 98 for five. Instead, Flintoff – dropped twice more – batted for nearly five and a half hours for an unbeaten century as England made 285, their innings lasting into the fourth afternoon. Despite following on 466 adrift, they were never in serious danger as Trescothick and Vaughan put personally challenging series behind them with a first-wicket partnership of 182, Vaughan top-scoring with 140 as England ended the match on 422 for five.

Later that year, England did whitewash Lara's men 4–0 in the return series, the Antigua draw the only "blip" in an outstanding run of 11 wins in 12 Tests. West Indies won the ensuing Champions Trophy, beating England in the final, but problems relating to player image-rights and the Caribbean's complicated cricketing politics soon put paid to Lara's second spell as captain. It was under Chanderpaul's leadership that he achieved his next great milestone. In 2005, with an innings of 226 against Australia in Adelaide, Lara passed Allan Border's mark of 11,174 runs to become the highest run-scorer in Test cricket. He held that record until India's Sachin Tendulkar beat his final total of 11,953 a little under three years later. In 2006, Lara was reinstated for a third spell as West Indies captain but bowed out after the 2007 World Cup following further internal disputes, saying that his hands were tied in terms of selection. It was a sad finish to the career of a man who, in the judgement of many, was the greatest batsman of his generation.

Lara described getting back the record for the highest individual Test score as "destiny, I suppose", telling reporters: "It's hard to believe. Matthew Hayden must have played well against Zimbabwe. It doesn't matter who you play against. To score that amount of runs… I'm amazed to be here again. It's a great feeling." Just as Lara had rung Hayden after his innings, so Hayden returned the compliment. "I knew Lara would be holding court," he wrote. "Much like Warnie, Lara doesn't flutter around the room like a butterfly. Kings don't do that. They just set up camp and wait for people to pay homage. I could picture Lara at the back of the room, still in his whites with his West Indies cap on, feet up on a chair and regally puffing his giant cigar – out of the side of his mouth, of course. A king in his element – the only thing missing would be veil-wearing women wafting palm branches."

For some, the 400 sequel topped the original. Lara himself said that England's bowling was more disciplined in 2004, while Michael Atherton – although remembering the 375 as "a flawless innings, touched by genius" – inclined towards the latter performance. "Given the context, because he sensed the importance of the innings to West Indies cricket, because he still had the stamina and desire even though he was a decade older and, above all else, because he climbed Everest twice, this was a more significant achievement than ten years ago," he wrote. "Any man who goes into uncharted territory in sport automatically touches greatness." The *Daily Mirror's* Mike Walters said that the 400 was "the equivalent of Neil Armstrong walking on the moon and going back into space ten years later to set foot on Mars". Statistically, the two innings were strikingly similar, the 400 spanning 44 more balls, lasting 12 more minutes and containing two fewer fours and four more sixes (there were no sixes in the 375).

Asked if his 400 and 501 would ever be beaten, Lara said: "Records were made to be broken. A guy scored 499. People would have said, 'Who's going to get that?' I don't know if they will be broken, but it would be nice for cricket if someone else can get to those heights once more. You don't want to be

sitting on the record for 40, 50, 60 years. You want to see some
youngster come out and go after it and achieve it."

Lara has pinpointed India's Virat Kohli, Rohit Sharma and
Prithvi Shaw as possible contenders to take the Test record.
At the time of writing, it had been most seriously threatened
in 2006, when Mahela Jayawardene scored 374 for Sri Lanka
against South Africa in Colombo. Jayawardene was within
touching distance when suddenly surprised by a ball from
fast bowler Andre Nel that nipped back, kept low and bowled
him. Earlier, the diminutive right-hander had shared in a
first-class record partnership of 624 with Kumar Sangakkara,
who scored 287. Jayawardene had to content himself with an
innings victory and the consolation of having beaten Sanath
Jayasuriya's national record of 340. "I am pretty happy with
what I've done," he said. "Brian Lara has set a score which is
not easy to break. One day somebody will."

*So near and yet so far: Sri Lanka's Mahela Jayawardene is congratulated
and consoled by South Africa's Jacques Rudolph after falling 27 short of
beating Lara's score at Colombo in 2006.*

Lara's recovery of the record was only the tenth time that cricket's greatest batting accolade has changed hands. The record for the best bowling figures in a Test innings has done so nine times – three times in the inaugural Test in 1877 through to Jim Laker's ten for 53 for England against Australia at Old Trafford in 1956, when it rather came to an abrupt standstill. Again, at the time of writing, there has been only one Test match ten-for since then – Anil Kumble's ten for 74 for India against Pakistan at Delhi in 1999. The comparative lack of aura surrounding the bowling record perhaps betrays Laker's pre-eminence and the fact that scoreboards have not always carried the bowler's figures, whereas the batsman's tally has always been an essential feature, giving time for drama and tension to develop.

Jayawardene's comment that Lara's score is not easy to break highlights the factors needed to scale such heights. As well as the batsman's ability and form, his health, fitness and general motivation, the quality of bowling is clearly important along with the pitch, weather and match situation and where the game is being played (the record is much more likely to fall on a "dead" pitch outside England, for example, than on an archetypal English seamer). Luck is also a key component; had umpire Darrell Hair been persuaded by an audible noise – but no discernible deflection – when the ball from Harmison passed Lara's bat before he'd scored a run at Antigua in 2004, the record would have remained with Hayden. Indeed, a characteristic of all the record innings, to a greater or lesser extent, is that they had their elements of fortune. Even Lara's "flawless innings" of 375, in the gracious words of opposing captain Atherton, almost saw him hit his wicket in playing the shot that took him past Sobers. One shudders, in fact, at the appalling thought of Lara's off bail coming off completely as his pad brushed against the stumps in the act of pulling that historic four. The record breakers have benefited from dropped catches, timeless Tests, weak opponents, flat pitches, even seasick bowlers. Not only do the stars have to shine, the stars must also align.

Will Lara's record be broken? By the time you read this it might have been, but it will be increasingly difficult to keep pushing the envelope. One-day cricket has produced batsmen capable of remarkable feats of fast scoring, leading to more aggressive, dynamic strokeplay in the longer formats too. The bats themselves get sweeter and sweeter, the boundaries seemingly ever smaller, and the players today are fine-tuned athletes with all the power and fitness needed. However, they generally have less desire to "bat time" than their predecessors, nor the same technical grounding to do so. First-class cricket is shrinking in quality/quantity, not least in England's marginalised County Championship, in which the top players – both domestic and overseas – rarely feature in this era of central contracts and changing priorities. The desire of some for four-day Tests – to cram in yet more white-ball games – would clearly make the task even tougher. Already administrators' endless pursuit of the bottom line is reducing cricket to matches of 100 balls per side and less, with five-day contests inconvenient to the powers that be. The increase in T20 franchise cricket – and the huge financial rewards for players – increases, too, the scope for player-drain from Test cricket and potential challengers to the record. Players are becoming white-ball specialists, naturally following the trail of cash. Faced with the choice between bags of brass and carving their name into *Wisden's* Test records section, the old yellow book appeals more to the romantics, perhaps, than the pragmatists. Technology is also a significant factor when pondering the scope for record attempts. The Decision Review System (DRS), introduced in 2009, although guarding against the possibility of batsmen being "sawn off" by umpires, also means that those thin snicks and marginal lbw calls of yesteryear, when batsmen might have received the benefit of doubt, are now more likely to go for the bowlers. Over-rates are also pertinent, with crowds routinely robbed of a full day's play and batsmen of potentially run-filled overs. That said, going into the year 2020, of the 31 triple-centuries in Test cricket, 16 had come since 2000 and 20 since 1990, although the caveat is that more than half of all Test cricket has been played since 1990.

Perhaps the biggest factor against challengers now is the introduction in 2019 of the World Test Championship. Designed to give greater context to series, with points available for each game, it is, by any measure, no saviour of Test cricket at all, thereby taking its place alongside four-day fixtures, pink balls and whatever else is dreamt up next. However, for all its faults and flawed points system, enough to befuddle Socrates, it does at least encourage fewer dead rubber games à la Antigua 2004 and puts more emphasis on gaining positive results. Consequently, the capacity for huge individual scores and what might be termed self-indulgent record pursuit is reduced, not to say frowned upon in an increasingly professional, results-driven age.

This was highlighted in late 2019 when Australia's David Warner was denied a shot at Lara's record. Warner was on 335 against Pakistan in Adelaide when his captain, Tim Paine, declared with the total on 589 for three around 40 minutes before dinner on day two of the pink-ball Test. Explaining the move, which Warner was privy to and fully behind,

Paine – cognisant of a poor weather forecast – said: "We're here to win Test matches, and with the Test Championship now there is 60 points on the line. If we kept batting and it rained for a day, we would be kicking ourselves." By day's end, Australia had reduced a poor Pakistan team to 96 for six. They went on to win by an innings and 48 runs with over a day to spare.

Paine's decision, although emblematic of the team-first ethos, was backed and criticised equally. Most understood that winning came first, although a general sense of disappointment prevailed (tempered, perhaps, by Warner's Marmite personality). Lara was also sorry for Warner, believing that Australia might have given him at least 12 overs before dinner to have a dart. By incredible coincidence he was in Adelaide himself and on his way back to the ground after returning to his hotel to get changed following corporate duties. In fact, Lara was readying himself to walk out on to the field, Sobers-style, to offer his congratulations. "It would have been amazing to walk out there," he said. Instead, Paine pulled out after giving Warner the opportunity to go past Don Bradman and Mark Taylor's evocative figure of 334.

Warner's triple-hundred – and the reaction to it – put the record back in the spotlight. It was noticeable how social media engaged with the rights and wrongs of Paine's decision; the romance of the record resonated with the Twitter generation as much as with those generations which associate the word "twitter" with chirping sounds. Only a select group of batsmen have worn the proud crown of the highest individual score in Test cricket since the first coronation in 1877. The bar set by Charles Bannerman all those years ago – before Test cricket was even officially recognised – has since been lifted to improbable heights, ready to be raised once more.

West Indies v England

Played at Antigua Recreation Ground, St John's, Antigua, on 10, 11, 12, 13, 14 April, 2004.

Toss: West Indies. Result: Match drawn.

WEST INDIES

C. H. Gayle c and b Batty	69	†R. D. Jacobs not out	107
D. Ganga lbw b Flintoff	10	B 4, lb 5, w 2, nb 5	16
*B. C. Lara not out	400		
R. R. Sarwan c Trescothick b Harmison	90	1/33 (2) (5 wkts dec, 202 overs)	751
R. L. Powell c Hussain b S. P. Jones	23	2/98 (1) 3/330 (4)	
R. O. Hinds c and b Batty	36	4/380 (5) 5/469 (6)	

T. L. Best, P. T. Collins, C. D. Collymore and F. H. Edwards did not bat.

Hoggard 18–2–82–0; Harmison 37–6–92–1; Flintoff 35–8–109–1; S. P. Jones 29–0–146–1;
Batty 52–4–185–2; Vaughan 13–0–60–0; Trescothick 18–3–68–0.

ENGLAND

M. E. Trescothick c Jacobs b Best	16	– c Sarwan b Edwards	88
*M. P. Vaughan c Jacobs b Collins	7	– c Jacobs b Sarwan	140
M. A. Butcher b Collins	52	– c Gayle b Hinds	61
N. Hussain b Best	3	– b Hinds	56
G. P. Thorpe c Collins b Edwards	10	– not out	23
A. Flintoff not out	102	– c Lara b Sarwan	14
†G. O. Jones b Edwards	38	– not out	10
G. J. Batty c Gayle b Collins	8		
M. J. Hoggard c Jacobs b Collins	1		
S. P. Jones lbw b Hinds	11		
S. J. Harmison b Best	5		
B 1, lb 5, w 4, nb 22	32	B 4, lb 7, w 3, nb 16	30

1/8 (2) 2/45 (1) 3/54 (4)	(99 overs) 285	1/182 (1) (5 wkts, 137 overs) 422
4/98 (3) 5/98 (5) 6/182 (7)		2/274 (2) 3/366 (3)
7/205 (8) 8/229 (9) 9/283 (11) 10/285 (10)		4/387 (4) 5/408 (6)

In the first innings S. P. Jones, when 11, retired hurt at 277-8 and resumed at 283-9.

Collins 26–4–76–4; Edwards 18–3–70–2; Collymore 19–5–45–0; Best 10.3–3–37–3; Hinds
17.3–7–29–1; Sarwan 7–0–18–0; Gayle 1–0–4–0. *Second innings* — Best 16–1–57–0; Edwards
20–2–81–1; Collymore 18–3–58–0; Powell 8–0–36–0; Hinds 38–8–83–2; Gayle 17–6–36–0;
Sarwan 12–2–26–2; Collins 8–2–34–0.

Umpires: Aleem Dar and D. B. Hair.   Third umpire: B. R. Doctrove.

Referee: M. J. Procter. J. J. Crowe replaced Procter on the fourth day.

Statistical Appendix

The Record Holders

Charles Bannerman

Full name: *Charles Bannerman*

Born: *July 3, 1851, Woolwich, Kent*

Died: *August 20, 1930, Surry Hills, Sydney*

Major teams: *Australia, New South Wales*

Role: *Right-hand batsman*

First-class career: *1870-71 to 1887-88*

Test record: *Matches 3, Innings 6, Not Outs 2, Runs 239, Average 59.75, Highest Score 165*, 100s 1, 50s 0; Wickets 0; Catches 0*

First-class record: *Matches 44, Innings 84, Not Outs 6, Runs 1,687, Average 21.62, Highest Score 165*, 100s 1, 50s 9; Wickets 0; Catches 20*

Billy Murdoch

Full name: *William Lloyd Murdoch*

Born: *October 18, 1854, Sandhurst, Victoria*

Died: *February 18, 1911, Melbourne, Victoria*

Major teams: *Australia, England, New South Wales, Sussex, London County*

Role: *Right-hand batsman*

First-class career: *1875-76 to 1904*

Test record: *Matches 19, Innings 34, Not Outs 5, Runs 908, Average 31.31, Highest Score 211, 100s 2, 50s 1; Wickets 0; Catches 14, Stumpings 1*

First-class record: *Matches 391, Innings 679, Not Outs 48, Runs 16,953, Average 26.86, Highest Score 321, 100s 19, 50s 85; Wickets 10, Average 43.00, Best Bowling 2-11; Catches 218, Stumpings 24*

"Tip" Foster

Full name: *Reginald Erskine Foster*

Born: *April 16, 1878, Malvern, Worcestershire*

Died: *May 13, 1914, Brompton, Kensington, London*

Major teams: *England, Oxford University, Worcestershire*

Role: *Right-hand batsman*

First-class career: *1897 to 1912*

Test record: *Matches 8, Innings 14, Not Outs 1, Runs 602, Average 46.30, Highest Score 287, 100s 1, 50s 1; Wickets 0; Catches 13*

First-class record: *Matches 139, Innings 234, Not Outs 17, Runs 9,076, Average 41.82, Highest Score 287, 100s 22, 50s 41; Wickets 25, Average 46.12, Best Bowling 3-54; Catches 178*

Andy Sandham

Full name: *Andrew Sandham*

Born: *July 6, 1890, Streatham, London*

Died: *April 20, 1982, Westminster, London*

Major teams: *England, Surrey*

Role: *Right-hand batsman*

First-class career: *1911 to 1937-38*

Test record: *Matches 14, Innings 23, Not Outs 0, Runs 879, Average 38.21, Highest Score 325, 100s 2, 50s 3; Wickets 0; Catches 4*

First-class record: *Matches 643, Innings 1,000, Not Outs 79, Runs 41,284, Average 44.82, Highest Score 325, 100s 107, 50s 207; Wickets 18, Average 31.11, Best Bowling 3-27; Catches 159*

Don Bradman

Full name: *Donald George Bradman*

Born: *August 27, 1908, Cootamundra, New South Wales*

Died: *February 25, 2001, Kensington Park, Adelaide, South Australia*

Major teams: *Australia, New South Wales, South Australia*

Role: *Right-hand batsman*

First-class career: *1927-28 to 1948-49*

Test record: *Matches 52, Innings 80, Not Outs 10, Runs 6,996, Average 99.94, Highest Score 334, 100s 29, 50s 13; Wickets 2, Average 36.00, Best Bowling 1-8; Catches 32*

First-class record: *Matches 234, Innings 338, Not Outs 43, Runs 28,067, Average 95.14, Highest Score 452*, 100s 117, 50s 69; Wickets 36, Average 37.97, Best Bowling 3-35; Catches 131, Stumpings 1*

Wally Hammond

Full name: *Walter Reginald Hammond*

Born: *June 19, 1903, Buckland, Dover, Kent*

Died: *July 1, 1965, Kloof, Natal*

Major teams: *England, Gloucestershire*

Role: *Right-hand batsman, right-arm fast-medium bowler*

First-class career: *1920 to 1951*

Test record: *Matches 85, Innings 140, Not Outs 16, Runs 7,249, Average 58.45, Highest Score 336*, 100s 22, 50s 24; Wickets 83, Average 37.80, Best Bowling 5-36; Catches 110*

First-class record: *Matches 634, Innings 1,005, Not Outs 104, Runs 50,551, Average 56.10, Highest Score 336*, 100s 167, 50s 185; Wickets 732, Average 30.58, Best Bowling 9-23; Catches 820, Stumpings 3*

Len Hutton

Full name: *Leonard Hutton*

Born: *June 23, 1916, Fulneck, Pudsey, Yorkshire*

Died: *September 6, 1990, Kingston-upon-Thames, Surrey*

Major teams: *England, Yorkshire*

Role: *Right-hand batsman, occasional leg-spin bowler*

First-class career: *1934 to 1960*

Test record: *Matches 79, Innings 138, Not Outs 15, Runs 6,971, Average 56.67, Highest Score 364, 100s 19, 50s 33; Wickets 3, Average 77.33, Best Bowling 1-2; Catches 57*

First-class record: *Matches 513, Innings 814, Not Outs 91, Runs 40,140, Average 55.51, Highest Score 364, 100s 129, 50s 179; Wickets 173, Average 29.51, Best Bowling 6-76; Catches 401*

Garry Sobers

Full name: *Garfield St Aubrun Sobers*

Born: *July 28, 1936, Bay Land, St Michael, Barbados*

Major teams: *West Indies, Barbados, Nottinghamshire, South Australia*

Role: *Left-hand batsman, left-arm fast/medium/slow bowler*

First-class career: *1952-53 to 1974*

Test record: *Matches 93, Innings 160, Not Outs 21, Runs 8,032, Average 57.78, Highest Score 365*, 100s 26, 50s 30; Wickets 235, Average 34.03, Best Bowling 6-73; Catches 109*

First-class record: *Matches 383, Innings 609, Not Outs 93, Runs 28,314, Average 54.87, Highest Score 365*, 100s 86, 50s 121; Wickets 1,043, Average 27.74, Best Bowling 9-49; Catches 405*

Matthew Hayden

Full name: *Matthew Lawrence Hayden*

Born: *October 29, 1971, Kingaroy, Queensland*

Major teams: *Australia, Queensland, Hampshire, Northamptonshire*

Role: *Left-hand batsman*

First-class career: *1991-92 to 2008-09*

Test record: *Matches 103, Innings 184, Not Outs 14, Runs 8,625, Average 50.73, Highest Score 380, 100s 30, 50s 29; Wickets 0; Catches 128*

First-class record: *Matches 295, Innings 515, Not Outs 47, Runs 24,603, Average 52.57, Highest Score 380, 100s 79, 50s 100; Wickets 17, Average 39.47, Best Bowling 3-10; Catches 296*

Brian Lara

Full name: *Brian Charles Lara*

Born: *May 2, 1969, Cantaro, Santa Cruz, Trinidad*

Major teams: *West Indies, Trinidad & Tobago, Warwickshire*

Role: *Left-hand batsman*

First-class career: *1987-88 to 2007-08*

Test record: *Matches 131, Innings 232, Not Outs 6, Runs 11,953, Average 52.88, Highest Score 400*, 100s 34, 50s 48; Wickets 0; Catches 164*

First-class record: *Matches 261, Innings 440, Not Outs 13, Runs 22,156, Average 51.88, Highest Score 501*, 100s 65, 50s 88; Wickets 4, Average 104.00, Best Bowling 1-1; Catches 320*

Author's Note/Acknowledgements

My thanks to Charlotte Croft, Sarah Skipper and Steven Lynch at Bloomsbury; to agent David Luxton; and to my old friend Peter Wynne-Thomas, the Nottinghamshire County Cricket Club librarian, for kindly checking the end result. It's amazing what Peter will do if you bribe him with a lunch of his favourite ham, egg and chips (plus half a Guinness, of course) in the Trent Bridge Inn on the edge of England's greatest ground. How anyone can be as lucid and spry in his 87th year is beyond me; perhaps the half of Guinness is the secret.

For help with the first three chapters especially (Messrs Bannerman, Murdoch and Foster), I am indebted to the *Trove* newspaper archive in Australia, a magnificent online resource which I would recommend to anyone foolish enough to spend countless hours researching and writing a book. Ditto the British newspaper archive and its vast gateway to publications which, in many cases, are sadly no more but still yield their treasures from beyond the tomb. *The Times*, *Daily Telegraph* and *Guardian* archives were also invaluable, as was that of the *Jamaica Gleaner*.

It will astonish no one in the cricket writing racket that David Frith, the eminent author/historian, got to Andy Sandham before "Sandy" passed away, resulting in several helpful nuggets from an interview he conducted with him over a pint or three in a smoky pub in Clapham in 1978. The magazine that Frith founded and edited, *Wisden Cricket Monthly*, which this author vividly remembers delivering – but only after sneakily reading – on his paper round as a young lad was another helpful resource, as was *The Cricketer* magazine, which also got to "Sandy" before it was too late. The three surviving record-holders, Garry Sobers, Matthew Hayden and Brian Lara, have written and spoken extensively about their innings and I am grateful for such recollections in what, I hope, is a tribute to them and their historic performances.

We are fortunate, in this digital era, that the last three innings featured – Lara's 375, Hayden's 380 and Lara's 400 – are richly preserved and available to watch on YouTube. The Sky/Channel Nine coverage was extremely helpful, as were various snippets of insight on the BBC Sport website. For help with the reproduction of score-cards I am obliged to Harriet Monkhouse, Charles Davis and Ross English. My thanks also to the usual suspects of ESPNcricinfo and Cricket Archive for the outstanding statistical services which pretty much underpin all cricket books/cricket journalism these days, as well as to my faithful employers, *The Yorkshire Post*, who have tolerated my ramblings now for more years than they would care to be reminded. A hat tip, while we're at it, to Boddingtons Bitter, innumerable cans of which – never mind the odd half of Guinness – sustained me through the lonely endeavour.

Someone asked, as I was finishing the book, which record innings was, in my humble opinion, the best, or at least my favourite. It's a tricky question, not least in the absence of a time machine to conveniently drop in, say, on Headingley 1930 or Sabina Park 1958 to see Bradman/Sobers in full cry. And although many sage observers consider Lara's 400 to have been a greater achievement than his 375, which it may well have been for all I know, I nevertheless find myself drawn, perhaps sentimentally, to that 375 and an innings played by a man I regard as the greatest batsman of my cricket-watching experience.

It is interesting that in the winter of his life Don Bradman identified Sachin Tendulkar as the modern master who most reminded him of himself in terms of technique. The comparison is striking if one contrasts video footage, but it has always struck me that Lara is actually the closest thing that cricket has seen to Bradman in terms of appetite/ability to churn out huge scores. For Lara to have broken the Test and first-class records within a few weeks in 1994 was, as the former Yorkshire and England fast bowler Fred Trueman might have emphasised, "un-be-liev-able", and I vividly recall as a young man following the 375 on *Test Match Special* in a state of nervous excitement, marvelling at the extraordinary events unfolding some 4,000 miles away. That Lara passed Sobers's mark after the longest gap between all the record innings (36 years), and with the great Sobers present at the stadium to add to the enormous weight of expectation, was a truly sensational achievement by a young man of 24, and that's before we even consider the innings itself.

It has been, quite frankly, an emotional experience to watch back footage of the 375, the 380 and the 400 and to delve into all these record performances, some of them so distant that it felt like trying to piece together details about the "Big Bang". For in an era in which cricket is a slave to the lowest common denominator as never before, its greatest format must be cherished and celebrated for all it is worth.

Bibliography

Arlott, John, *The Echoing Green*, Longmans, Green and Co., 1952

Arlott, John, *Jack Hobbs: Profile of 'The Master'*, Murray, 1981

Atherton, Mike, *Opening Up: My Autobiography*, Hodder & Stoughton, 2002

Bannister, Jack, *Brian Lara: The Story of a Record-Breaking Year*, Stanley Paul, 1994

Bannister, Jack, *The Innings of My Life*, Headline, 1995

Barker, Ralph, *Ten Great Innings*, Chatto & Windus, 1964

Barrett, Norman, (ed.), *The Daily Telegraph Chronicle of Cricket*, Guinness, 1994

Baxter, Peter, (ed.), *Test Match Special: 50 Not Out*, BBC Books, 2007

Berry, Scyld, (ed.), *The Observer on Cricket: An Anthology of the Best Cricket Writing*, Unwin Hyman, 1987

Booth, Keith, *His Own Enemy: The Rise and Fall of Edward Pooley*, Belmont Books, 2000

Bowes, Bill, *Express Deliveries*, Stanley Paul, 1949

Bradman, Don, *My Cricketing Life*, Stanley Paul, 1938

Bradman, Don, *Farewell to Cricket*, Hodder & Stoughton, 1950

Brogden, Stanley; Arlott, John, *The First Test Match: England v Australia 1877*, Phoenix House Limited, 1950

Cardus, Neville, *Cardus on Cricket*, Sportsman's Book Club, 1949

Cardus, Neville, *Cardus in the Covers*, Souvenir Press, 1978

Cardus, Neville, *Play Resumed with Cardus*, Souvenir Press, 1979

Carr, A. W., *Cricket With The Lid Off*, Hutchinson & Co., 1935

Cashman, Richard, (ed.), *The Oxford Companion to Australian Cricket*, Oxford University Press, 1997

Cashman, Richard, *The Demon Fred Spofforth*, Walla Walla Press, 2014

Chignell, W. R., *A History of the Worcestershire County Cricket Club, 1844-1950*, Littlebury & Co., 1951

Cozier, Tony, *The West Indies: Fifty Years Of Test Cricket*, Angus & Robertson, 1978

Douglas, Christopher, *Douglas Jardine: Spartan Cricketer*, Methuen, 2002

Flintoff, Andrew, *Being Freddie: My Story So Far*, Hodder & Stoughton, 2005

Foot, David, *Wally Hammond: The Reasons Why*, Robson Books, 1998

Frith, David, *The Fast Men*, Corgi, 1977

Frith, David, *Bodyline Autopsy*, Aurum, 2002

Frith, David, *Frith on Cricket*, Great Northern Books, 2010

Frith, David, *Frith's Encounters*, Von Krumm Publishing, 2014

Fry, C. B., *Life Worth Living*, Eyre and Spottiswoode, 1939

Fuller, James, *Brian Lara: An unauthorised biography*, Signal, 2013

Giffen, George, *With Bat and Ball*, Ward, Lock & Co., 1898

Haigh, Gideon, *Game for Anything: Writings on Cricket*, Aurum, 2005

Haigh, Gideon, *Silent Revolutions: Writings on Cricket History*, Aurum, 2007

Haigh, Gideon, *Stroke of Genius: Victor Trumper and the Shot that Changed Cricket*, Simon & Schuster, 2016

Hamilton, Duncan, (ed.), *Sweet Summers: The Classic Cricket Writing of JM Kilburn*, Great Northern Books, 2008

Hamilton, Duncan, *Harold Larwood*, Quercus, 2009

Hammond, Walter, *Cricket My Destiny*, Stanley Paul, 1946

Hammond, Walter, *Cricket My World*, Stanley Paul, 1948

Hayden, Matthew, *Standing My Ground*, Aurum, 2011

Haygarth, Arthur, *Marylebone Club's Continuation of Frederick Lillywhite's Cricket Scores and Biographies for 1877 to 1878 – Volume XIV*, Longman's & Co., 1895

Hoult, Nick, (ed.), *The Daily Telegraph Book of Cricket*, Aurum, 2007

Howat, Gerald, *Walter Hammond*, Allen & Unwin, 1984

Howat, Gerald, *Len Hutton*, Heinemann Kingswood, 1988

Hussain, Nasser, *Playing With Fire*, Penguin, 2004

Hutton, Len, *Cricket is My Life*, Hutchinson & Co., 1949

Hutton, Len, *Just My Story*, Hutchinson & Co., 1956

Hutton, Len, *Fifty Years in Cricket*, Stanley Paul, 1984

Inglis, Gordon, *Sport & Pastime in Australia*, Methuen & Co. Ltd, 1912

James, Alfred, *Charles Bannerman: Australia's Premier Batsman*, The Cricket Publishing Company, 2016

Langer, Justin, *Seeing The Sunrise*, Allen & Unwin, 2008

Lara, Brian, *Beating The Field: My Own Story*, Partridge Press, 1995

Larwood, Harold; Perkins, Kevin, *The Larwood Story*, Bonpara Pty, 1982

Manley, Michael, *A History of West Indies Cricket*, Guild Publishing, 1998

Mason, Ronald, *Walter Hammond*, Hollis & Carter, 1962

McKinstry, Leo, *Jack Hobbs: England's Greatest Cricketer*, Yellow Jersey, 2011

Mills, Robert, *Field of Dreams: Headingley 1890-2001*, Great Northern Books, 2001

Moyes, A. G., *Australian Cricket: A History*, Angus & Robertson, 1959

Murdoch, William L., *Cricket: With Illustrations*, George Routledge & Sons Limited, 1893

Oborne, Peter, *Wounded Tiger: A History of Cricket in Pakistan*, Simon & Schuster, 2014

Parkinson, Michael, *Michael Parkinson on Cricket*, Hodder & Stoughton, 2002

Pearson, Harry, *Connie: The Marvellous Life of Learie Constantine*, Little, Brown, 2017

Pullin, A. W., *Alfred Shaw, Cricketer: His Career and Reminiscences*, Cassell, 1902

Rae, Simon, *W. G. Grace: A Life*, Faber and Faber, 1998

Reese, T. W., *New Zealand Cricket 1914-1933*, Whitcombe & Tombs Limited, 1936

Robertson-Glasgow, R. C., *Cricket Prints: Some Batsmen and Bowlers 1920-1940*, T. Werner Laurie, 1943

Robertson-Glasgow, R. C., *More Cricket Prints: Some Batsmen and Bowlers 1920-1945*, T. Werner Laurie, 1948

Robinson, Ray, *On Top Down Under: Australia's Cricket Captains*, Cassell Australia, 1975

Rosenwater, Irving, *Sir Donald Bradman: A Biography*, Batsford, 1978

Ross, Gordon, *A History Of West Indies Cricket*, Arthur Barker Ltd., 1976

Scovell, Brian, *Brian Lara: Cricket's Troubled Genius*, Stadia, 2007

Searle, Andrew, *S. F. Barnes: His Life and Times*, Empire Publications, 1997

Shaw A.; Shrewsbury A., *Shaw & Shrewsbury's Team in Australia 1884-85*, Shaw & Shrewsbury, 1885

Sobers, Gary, *My Most Memorable Matches*, Stanley Paul, 1984

Sobers, Garry, *Twenty Years at the Top*, Macmillan, 1988

Sobers, Garry, *My Autobiography*, Headline, 2002

Sutcliffe, Herbert, *For England and Yorkshire*, Edward Arnold & Co., 1935

Swanton, Jim; Plumptre, George, (ed.), *Back Page Cricket: A Century of Newspaper Coverage*, Macdonald Queen Anne Press, 1987

Thomson, A. A., *Hirst and Rhodes*, The Epworth Press, 1959

Vaughan, Michael, *Calling The Shots: The Captain's Story*, Hodder & Stoughton, 2005

Warner, P. F., *How We Recovered The Ashes* (Centenary Edition), Methuen, 2003

Williams, Marcus, (ed.), *Double Century: 200 Years of Cricket in The Times*, Collins, 1985

Wisden Cricketers' Almanack, various editions

Wyatt, R. E. S., *Three Straight Sticks*, Stanley Paul, 1951

Index